D0935325

IN THE NAME OF GOD, GO!

BOOKS EDITED BY WM. ROGER LOUIS

(with Prosser Gifford) *Britain and Germany in Africa* (1967)

(with Prosser Gifford) *France and Britain in Africa* (1971)

National Security and International Trusteeship in the Pacific (1972)

(with William S. Livingston) *Australia, New Zealand and the Pacific Islands Since the First World War* (1979)

The Origins of the Second World War: A. J. P. Taylor and His Critics (1972)

Imperialism: The Robinson and Gallagher Controversy (1976)

(with Prosser Gifford) *The Transfer of Power in Africa* (1982)

(with Prosser Gifford) *Decolonization and African Independence* (1988)

(with Hedley Bull) *The Special Relationship: Anglo-American Relations Since 1945* (1986)

(with Roger Owen) *Suez 1956: The Crisis and Its Consequences* (1989)

(with Robert W. Stookey) *The End of the Palestine Mandate* (1986)

(with James A. Bill) *Musaddiq, Iranian Nationalism, and Oil* (1988)

(with Robert A. Fernea) *The Iraqi Revolution of 1958* (1991)

(with Robert Blake) *Churchill* (1993)

*Amery and Churchill survey, in the latter's phrase,
"The vast reservoir of Indian manpower."
Despite such light-hearted phrases, both Churchill
and Amery regarded Indian military assistance as vital to the winning
of the war. The two Indian leaders are Hon. Sir Ramaswani Mudaliar
and His Highness the Maharajah Jam Sahib of Nawanagar.*

IN THE NAME OF GOD, GO!

Leo Amery and the British Empire
in the Age of Churchill

WM. ROGER LOUIS

W·W·NORTON & COMPANY
New York   London

The text of this book is composed in Times Roman
with the display set in Perpetua
Composition by PennSet Inc.
Manufacturing by Courier Companies, Inc.
Book design by Jacques Chazaud

Library of Congress Cataloging-in-Publication Data

Louis, William Roger
In the name of God, go! : Leo Amery and the British Empire in the
age of Churchill / by Wm. Roger Louis.
p.   cm.
Includes index.
1. Amery, L. S. (Leopold Stennett), 1873–1955.   2. Great Britain—
Colonies—Administration—History—20th century.   3. Great Britain—
Politics and government—20th century.   4. Statesmen—Great
Britain—Biography.   I. Title.
DA566.9.A44L68   1992
941.084′092—dc20
[B]   91-47548

ISBN 0-393-03393-7

W.W. Norton & Company, Inc., 500 Fifth Avenue, New York, N.Y. 10110
W.W. Norton & Company Ltd., 10 Coptic Street, London WC1A 1PU

1 2 3 4 5 6 7 8 9 0

For Dagmar

Contents

9

Preface

This study had its origins in the Chichele Lectures at All Souls College, Oxford, in May 1990. The lectures were part of a larger series on 'All Souls in the Twentieth Century'. My purpose at the time was to comment on Amery and the College against the larger background of the British Empire. That perspective is still present, but the theme has now become Amery's part in the shaping of British imperialism from the turn of the century to the end of the Second World War. The result should not be mistaken for a biographical inquiry, though I have tried to place Amery in his historical era and to portray his buoyant personality. My aim is to describe the development of his economic and military ideas, the extent of his political influence, and the significance of the contrast in his outlook on India and other matters with that of Winston Churchill.

I shall not attempt to list my friends at St. Antony's and All Souls as well as the University of Texas who have helped me with the manuscript, but I make exceptions of Sarvepalli Gopal and Albert Hourani who have given me, as usual, extraordinary advice. I wish also to thank some others who have assisted me, including John Barnes, Robert Blake, William R. Braisted, Donald Cameron Watt, Robert Holland, Ronald Hyam, Alaine Low, Peter Lyon, and Norman Rose. My debt to the two volumes of *The Leo Amery Diaries*, edited by John Barnes and David Nicholson, will be apparent, but I should mention that when the manuscript diaries are especially relevant to my theme I have sometimes given the reference to the original manuscripts rather than to the published diaries. I am especially grateful to Julian Amery for allowing me to study his father's papers.

My main source of information and interpretation is the material in the Amery Papers, but the book is based also on other private papers and archives, as listed on pp. 13–14. I thank the librarians and archivists who have helped me, as well as the holders of copyright.

Abbreviations and Location of Manuscript Sources

Amery Papers. Papers of Leopold Amery, privately held.

Avon Papers. Papers of Lord Avon (Sir Anthony Eden), Birmingham University Library, Birmingham.

Baldwin Papers. Papers of Stanley Baldwin, Cambridge University Library, Cambridge.

Beaverbrook Papers. Papers of Lord Beaverbrook, House of Lords Record Office, London.

Austin Chamberlain Papers. Papers of Sir Austin Chamberlain, Birmingham University Library, Birmingham.

Joseph Chamberlain Papers. Papers of Joseph Chamberlain, Birmingham University Library, Birmingham.

Neville Chamberlain Papers. Papers of Neville Chamberlain, Birmingham University Library, Birmingham.

Coupland Papers. Papers of Sir Reginald Coupland, Rhodes House, Oxford.

Curtis Papers. Papers of Lionel Curtis, Bodleian Library, Oxford.

Dawson Papers. Papers of Geoffrey Dawson, Bodleian Library, Oxford.

Sir Edward Grigg Papers. Papers of Sir Edward Grigg (Lord Altrincham), privately held.

P.J. Grigg Papers. Papers of P.J. Grigg, Churchill College, Cambridge.

Jebb Papers. Papers of Richard Jebb, Institute of Commonwealth Studies, London.

Law Papers. Papers of Andrew Bonar Law, House of Lords Record Office, London.

Liddell Hart Papers. Papers of Sir Basil Liddell Hart, King's College, London.

Linlithgow Papers. Papers of Lord Linlithgow, India Office Library, London.

George Lloyd Papers. Papers of Lord Lloyd, Churchill College, Cambridge.

Lloyd George Papers. Papers of David Lloyd George, House of Lords Record Office, London.

Mackinder Papers. Papers of Sir Halford Mackinder, Geography Library, Oxford.

Milner Papers. Papers of Lord Milner, Bodleian Library, Oxford.

Rhodes Trust Papers. Papers of the Rhodes Trust, Rhodes House, Oxford.

Round Table Papers. Papers of the Round Table, Bodleian Library, Oxford.

Simon Papers. Papers of Sir John Simon, Bodleian Library, Oxford.

Templewood Papers. Papers of Lord Templewood (Sir Samuel Hoare), Cambridge University, Cambridge.

All Souls Archives. Archives of All Souls College, Oxford.

India Office Records. India Office Library, London.

Public Record Office, London:
      CAB   Cabinet Office
      CO   Colonial Office
      FO   Foreign Office

Amery Diaries I & II: John Barnes and David Nicholson, eds., *The Leo Amery Diaries* (2 vols., London, 1980 and 1988).

My Political Life: L.S. Amery, *My Political Life* (3 vols., London, 1953–55).

IN THE NAME OF GOD, GO!

Introduction

'In the name of God, go!' was the utterance made by Leo
Amery to Neville Chamberlain, the Prime Minister, in a
fraught House of Commons in May 1940. He believed
that Chamberlain had placed the Royal Navy and the
British Empire as well as England herself in mortal jeop-
ardy. Amery spoke from the hard right of the Tory Party.
His powerful denunciation helped to bring about the fall
of the Chamberlain government and thus played a crucial
part in Churchill's becoming Prime Minister. He was quot-
ing the words Oliver Cromwell had used to dismiss the
Long Parliament some three hundred years earlier; but it
is probably true that Amery's memory as much as Crom-

well's is evoked whenever the phrase comes to mind. For a moment there appeared to be the possibility that Amery himself might become Prime Minister. It was certainly one of his ambitions. Though he was conspicuous by his small stature (he was only five feet four), he had abounding vitality and a vigorous mind. But he was not usually a compelling speaker. He had been a member of the House of Commons since 1911, had served as Secretary of State for the Colonies and Dominions, and had stood by Churchill in the quest for British rearmament in the 1930s. Amery became Churchill's Secretary of State for India in 1940. The break with Chamberlain was traumatic. Chamberlain had helped him secure his first Parliamentary seat. 'I will not deny that I have been deeply hurt by some of the things you have done & said which cut just because they came from an old friend', the dying Chamberlain wrote half-reproachfully and in sadness to Amery.[1]

Amery was Churchill's friend from school days. Churchill was one year his junior at Harrow. Their careers ran parallel, but, though they were friends and respected each other, they were never intimates. Robert Rhodes James has written perceptively that there was always 'a definite restraint' between them, 'a lack of warmth, a noticeable caution and reserve.'[2] The tension between them derived in part from the issue of Free Trade versus protection, which is one of three themes in this book. Churchill believed that the abolition of protective duties and the free exchange of goods had established England's greatness in the nineteenth century. Amery on the other hand protested against the social and economic injustices of *laissez-*

1. Chamberlain to Amery, 14 October 1940, Amery Papers.
2. Robert Rhodes James, *Churchill: A Study in Failure, 1900–1939* (Cleveland, 1970), p. 328.

faire. He held that the time had passed when the British could afford Free Trade in the face of economic challenges from the European nations and the United States. He favoured a system of protection known as 'Imperial Preference'—'Empire Preference' is perhaps a more readily comprehensible term—which he championed in the tradition of Joseph Chamberlain.[3] Amery's protectionist idea was to create a self-sufficient common market embracing the Empire and the Dominions. Had this economic programme been pursued with tenacity and political will, the British Empire and Commonwealth might have remained, in Amery's vision, a great power along with the United States.

The second theme is national freedom. The lesson that Amery drew from the Boer War was that subject peoples could not be held in the British Empire against their will. It was imperative that they be offered political equality as well as economic opportunity. Amery was representative of his age and did not believe that this grand design could be applied equally to the white Dominions and to black Africa; but he followed his intuition as well as the consequences of his own logic and worked towards India's independence in the Second World War. I have taken care to elaborate the details of the Amery-Churchill relationship over India during the war because Amery has been misrepresented as a reactionary, mainly from his identification with Churchill. Confronted by Churchill's bitter resistance to initiatives for political progress, Amery nevertheless pressed for Dominion status and independence for India within the Commonwealth. The issue of

3. The two phrases are interchangeable, but Amery consistently used the term 'Imperial Preference', in part because it was more acceptable in the Dominions, which had freed themselves from 'Empire' status.

India nearly broke their friendship. Amery believed that Churchill was to India as George III had been to the American colonies. Though recognizing Churchill's stature as a wartime leader, Amery saw—to borrow one of the passages in the diary quoted later—that 'India, or any form of self-government for coloured peoples, raises in him a wholly uncontrollable complex.' Churchill and Amery stood for two entirely different attitudes towards India and the Empire in general. To Churchill the British Empire, especially India, was an ornament of England's greatness and a reservoir of manpower. To Amery the Empire was not merely a source of pride but an ever-replenishing fountain of British power. He saw that the power of the British Empire would be increasingly challenged by European competitors as well as by the United States, and eventually by Japan.

The third theme is Amery as the philosopher and statesman of the Imperial movement in Britain. He was the disciple of Lord Milner, in Amery's view the greatest of Imperial statesmen, who held the Empire on steady course during the two critical periods of the Boer War and the latter half of the First World War. Amery himself became the theorist par excellence of British imperialism. He was a Fellow of All Souls College, Oxford, which to him represented the almost spiritual essence of the British Empire. Amery used All Souls as a sounding board of intellectual and expert advice. He and his circle of friends believed that the nation's resources had to be mobilized and used more effectively. He held that national efficiency required the transformation of the rickety nineteenth-century Empire into an effective Imperial union that would guarantee the defence of the Empire as a whole and would co-ordinate its economic development. The

Empire and Commonwealth would offer fields for investment and opportunities for trade as well as areas for emigration and settlement. The colonies and dependencies
in Africa, the Middle East, and Asia would be welded
together into federations and other larger units that would
offer an alternative to 'balkanization' into ethnic or other
components unable to stand on their own either economically or politically. Leo Amery led his generation in attempting to cast those ideas into a coherent and encompassing system of thought.

The questions asked by Amery are as perplexing today
as they were in his own time. How could the question of
communalism, which he recognized as the basic problem
in the Middle East and India, be reconciled with national
aspirations? Was there any way to prevent the fragmentation of India into ethnic and religious parts? Could an
'artificial' state such as Iraq, with diverse ethnic components and artificial boundaries, be held together indefinitely? If not, what were the alternatives? One thing for
sure was that the British had to do all they could to keep
the fragile Middle Eastern states within the orbit of western influence. Amery died in the year before the Suez
crisis of 1956, but there can be little doubt that he would
have advocated the continuation of the British military
operation against Nasser at any cost and a march on Cairo
to install a regime more friendly to the West. It is of course
speculative what attitude Amery might have adopted towards the conflict with Iraq in 1990–91, but if his past
record is any indication he would have applauded the
cooperation of the United States and Britain, and he
would have deplored stopping short of Baghdad. This at
least is the view held by his son, Julian, whose own ideas
demonstrate a remarkable consistency with those of his

father. Leo Amery was by no means jingoistic or aggressively patriotic, but he did believe that stability in the Middle East could only be maintained by the determination of the western powers to intervene whenever necessary to keep the peace and to protect western access to Middle Eastern oil. Whether one agrees with him or not, his ideas reverberate to the present.

Amery was also a gentile Zionist. Indeed he can be regarded as one of the fathers of the state of Israel. He adopted the cause of Zionism in 1917 because he believed that the Jews deserved a 'national home'; but, as will be seen, the Jewish national homeland would also serve British purposes. 'Our ultimate end', he once wrote, 'is clearly to make Palestine the centre of a western influence, using the Jews as we have used the Scots, to carry the English ideal through the Middle East and not merely to make an artificial oriental Hebrew enclave in an oriental country.'[4] He also regarded Palestine as a crossroads of the British Empire, where a Zionist presence would check French ambitions and help safeguard the Suez Canal. He thought at first that Arabs and Jews could live harmoniously under British tutelage on the model of South Africa and Canada. He later believed that partition and an independent Jewish state need not permanently alienate the Arabs. His optimism was misplaced, but it was characteristic of his ebullient spirit. It is noteworthy that towards the end of his life Amery warned the Israelis against the possible consequences of militant Zionism, but he never questioned his original decision to exert his influence in favour of the Zionist cause.

Amery was much concerned with the connection be-

4. Amery MS Diary, 26 July 1928.

tween economic strength and strategic aims. To him the question of 'decline' was relative to national resources and the will to exploit them effectively. There was a streak of political Darwinism in Amery's thought. The rise and fall of states would be determined not only by resources but also by skilled and inventive scientific management. As a military reformer, naval strategist, and economic theorist who wished Britain to retain and increase her competitiveness, he believed that her future as a world power would rest on industrial progress and colonial development. His economic ideas were sophisticated, but they were also representative of the time. He held that the British needed raw materials and colonial markets for which in exchange they could offer manufactured goods and services. He emerges as an archetypal figure who thought that governing élites—in his case assisted by the intellectual élite of All Souls—needed to master the principle of industrial and colonial development as they faced continuous change, competition, and war. He once remarked: 'Those people who have the industrial power and the power of invention and science will be able to defeat all others.'[5]

Amery in other words was a modernizing and aggressive reformer, aware of the tensions between domestic commitments and overseas defence, but, in the end, a believer in the proposition that Britain could afford both a welfare state and defence forces overseas. There is a logic to his position that is relevant to the present. He would not have subscribed to Paul Kennedy's view that the United States suffers from 'imperial overstretch', but he would certainly have insisted on keeping commitments in line with finan-

5. Quoted in Paul Kennedy, *The Rise and Fall of the Great Powers* (New York, 1987), p. 196.

cial resources. Expert management of the economy, however, was only part of the problem. He believed above all that lack of political will contributes to decline. 'Has Britain lost the will to govern?', he asked. A.P. Thornton has written: 'The day that England permitted her power to go out of fashion, that day her great history would end. Holding this conviction, the imperialist was assured that it was he alone who, in an age of shifting opinion and sentimentality, saw the world straight.' Amery fits Thornton's description.[6]

What then went wrong? The small size of the British Isles and the comparatively sparse endowment of resources put Britain at a natural disadvantage against Russia or the United States, or for that matter Germany. In Amery's own words, 'how can we with our forty millions of people compete against states nearly double our size?' The compelling answer was Imperial unity, but to the public it was a highly debatable proposition whether the corollary of protection would work to Britain's advantage. By the turn of the century, Britain was falling behind not merely in producing coal, iron, and steel but also in innovative electrical and chemical technologies.[7] Could the lead in industry and technology be recovered by protection or would protection lead to further stagnation? Anything that resembled a German *Zollverein* or Free Trade bloc would be met with resistance in the colonies because Free Trade within the British Empire would destroy local industries. The developing industries in the colonies would

6. A.P. Thornton, *The Imperial Idea and Its Enemies* (London, 1959), p. xiv.

7. See Aaron L. Friedberg, *The Weary Titan: Britain and the Experience of Relative Decline 1895–1905* (Princeton, 1988), especially chap. 2; and Jon Tetsuro Sumida, *In Defence of Naval Supremacy: Finance, Technology and British Naval Policy, 1889–1914* (Boston, 1989).

become 'stereotyped' or, as we would say today, dependent on the metropolitan economy. Amery answered this criticism by stating that Imperial Preference would be pragmatic and flexible. It would secure 'for the Empire the maximum of the external trade of each part, treating the degree of Protectionism or Free Trade established in that part as a purely local concern.'[8] This was a powerful explanation, but it did not command general acceptance until the Ottawa agreements of 1932. Imperial Preference proved to be an uphill battle all the way and was never a popular cause. Free Trade, Churchill used to say to Amery, was what made England great in the nineteenth century and should continue to be the basic principle of the British economy in the twentieth.

In Amery's judgement there was a complicating external influence that could, and in his view eventually did, lead to Britain's eclipse. No matter how efficiently the British might manage their own military and economic resources, the future of the world economy, and with it the fate of the British Empire, would depend on the evolving economic power of the United States. He held that the United States, consciously or unconsciously, hoped to destroy Imperial Preference and to reduce Britain to the status of an economic satellite. For example, he once wrote about Roosevelt's Secretary of State: 'Cordell Hull really represents mid-nineteenth century vision on economics, coupled no doubt with the desire to create an American export hegemony in the world.'[9] 'American *Le-*

---

8. Quoted in Alfred Gollin, *Balfour's Burden: Arthur Balfour and Imperial Preference* (London, 1965), p. 245.

9. Amery to Lord Linlithgow, 'Private', 25 January 1941, Amery Papers. Amery also reserved special venom for Sumner Welles, the Under Secretary of State who, Amery believed, wished to break up the British Empire to America's advantage.

bensraum' was the phrase Amery used during the Second World War to describe what he saw as the attempt by the United States to dominate the world economically and thereby politically. This is a view that is both contentious and ironic. Would he have eventually acknowledged that there are similarities between the old Victorian principles of Free Trade and indirect political influence, and the American principles of the open door and self-determination? The arguments in favour of Free Trade are most appealing when one is in an economically dominant position.

There is a Kiplingesque quality to some of Amery's thoughts on Empire, no doubt in part because Kipling was one of his friends. 'If we were an effective nation', Kipling once lamented to Amery, 'but we aren't. . . . All that sticks up out of the wreckage is that . . . we have stripped ourselves of defences.'[10] Amery left his mark on the rearmament movement of the 1930s just as throughout his career he had contributed significantly to military reform. But it is as an influential Colonial Secretary in the 1920s that he achieved his greatest success. He is remembered above all as one of the moving figures in the building of the institutions of the British Empire. His legacy was the Colonial Development Act of 1929, the first landmark of western economic assistance to the non-western world. He attempted to raise the standards of life of ordinary people in the colonies by agricultural development. He helped to secure education and health measures. He backed the building of roads, bridges, and hydro-electric works. It is not surprising, though it is certainly amusing, that he was known in Treasury circles as the Mad Mullah

10. Kipling to Amery, 29 October 1935, Amery Papers.

of colonial finance. He also contributed to the legal and administrative institutions of the colonial state—and, his critics would add, to the prison systems and the control of tribal areas by aerial bombardment.

One of Amery's books, *The Forward View*, published in 1935, is especially significant in pulling together the diverse areas of his thought. It is a systematic exposition of his views on the colonies, the economics of the interwar years, and Britain's destiny as an Imperial nation. It is also representative of his formal writings. But, though he wrote cogently, his books and speeches seldom conveyed his personality, which overflowed with energy and bonhomie. He once wrote to the Prime Minister, Stanley Baldwin, in 1927: 'I love office. I love the sense of getting things done, I love the comradeship of the Cabinet. . . .' It is also characteristic of his exuberance that in the same letter he did not hesitate to point out some of the faults of his friend Winston, who was, according to Amery, 'a brilliant talker and military strategist who is frankly incapable of understanding finance or the meaning of Empire development. . . .'[11] The interplay between Amery and Churchill forms a major part of this study.

11. Amery to Baldwin, 10 April 1927, Amery Papers.

27

The Empire is not external to any of the British nation. It is something like the Kingdom of Heaven within ourselves.

—LEO AMERY

I

All Souls, the British Empire, and World Power

1897–1918

I N THE LAST PHASE of his career, Leo Amery served as
Secretary of State for India 1940–45. It is therefore of
interest that he was born in 1873 in India, at Gorakhpur
in the then North-Western Provinces near the Himalayas.[1]
His father was the son of a British official in the Indian
Forest Department, his mother a Hungarian. His mother's
central European origin explains the un-English name of
Leopold as well as his own lifelong interest in the Austro-
Hungarian Empire. Amery was taken to England at the

1. For the details of Amery's life, see especially the editorial passages in
John Barnes and David Nicholson, eds., *The Leo Amery Diaries* (2 vols.,
London, 1980 and 1988).

age of three, never again to return to India. Though he often debated Indian issues, the subcontinent did not prove to be one of his central preoccupations until the Second World War. Sanskrit, however, engaged his linguistic imagination sufficiently for him to spend a year on it at Oxford.[2] He owed his interest in languages, as well as his early political and historical knowledge, to his mother. At various times and at various levels of proficiency, he knew German, French, Italian, Russian, Turkish, Hungarian, Serbian, and Bulgarian, as well as Latin and Greek. It is thus not surprising that he was eventually referred to as 'the multilingual Fellow of All Souls'.

He was educated at Harrow, where he held top place in examinations, and where he met Winston Churchill, who was one year younger. On their first encounter Churchill pushed him, fully clothed, into 'Ducker' (Harrowese for swimming pool). After Amery retaliated, Churchill apologized but observed that Amery was 'small'. ('My father, too', explained Churchill as he retrieved the situation, 'is small, though he also is a great man.')[3] Churchill of course became Prime Minister and Amery did not, though this was one of Amery's aspirations. It was sometimes said of him that he might have been Prime Minister had he been half a head taller and his speeches half an hour shorter. Though only five feet four, Amery was wiry and athletic. At Harrow he was a gymnast, at Oxford a cross-country runner, and throughout his life a mountaineer. He possessed stamina, intellectual and phys-

2. 'For a year I did Sanskrit, getting as far as some of the Mahabharata and the Hitopadesa.' L.S. Amery, *My Political Life* (3 vols., London, 1953–55), I, p. 49. He had been 'equally voluble' in both English and 'Hindustani' when he left India at the age of three. Ibid., p. 27. In 1895 he received a scholarship in Turkish from the Imperial Institute.

3. Ibid., p. 39.

ical. He held his own with Churchill in games no less than in the thrust of debate. Throughout their careers they found themselves opposed to each other on the issue of Free Trade and on the question of India but, as will be seen, both were Zionists.

Until the Second World War, Amery and Churchill collided on Indian affairs only sporadically. On Free Trade they clashed from the beginning and forever after. Churchill was a resolute Free Trader, in Amery's words, 'a firm believer in the legend that England's prosperity and greatness had been created by Free Trade, and that the abolition of the Corn Laws had given the people the blessings of cheap food.'[4] Churchill never deviated from this outlook, though after 1931 he tended to state his views less dogmatically. In trying to understand the reasons for such dedication to the cause of Free Trade, Amery in his memoirs paid tribute to Churchill's patriotism. In Amery's opinion the old-fashioned and outdated tradition of Free Trade had helped to shape Churchill's consciousness of the English nation:

> Churchill is a great English patriot—the greatest of our age. But his patriotism has always been for England; the England that fought Philip of Spain, Louis XIV and Napoleon in the past; the England that in his own lifetime overcame Kaiser Wilhelm and Hitler . . . England the home of political freedom, enhanced in prestige and power by an Empire of beneficent rule over subject peoples and incidentally also by a periphery of younger free nations sprung from her loins; but England still the starting point and the ultimate object of policy.[5]

4. Ibid., II, p. 504. The best analysis of Churchill's economic thought is by Peter Clarke, 'Churchill's Economic Ideas', in Robert Blake and W.R. Louis, eds., *Churchill* (Oxford and New York, 1993).

5. *My Political Life*, I, p. 196.

Amery's description was both perceptive and accurate. His own patriotism he described as radically different, in his own words, 'a wider patriotism, blended with and yet transcending our several national patriotisms'—the patriotisms of the United Kingdom, the British Empire, and what eventually became known as the Commonwealth, which he saw developing naturally as a result of common economic interest. This was the basis of Amery's lifelong commitment to Imperial Preference, which he believed would be the enduring source of British power throughout the world. 'In carrying out the policy of Empire Preference boldly and to its fullest logical conclusions', Amery once wrote, 'we shall find ourselves once again taking the lead in shaping the course of world economics in the coming century as we did in the last. . . .'[6]

By Imperial Preference he meant a form of protection by which the Empire and Dominions would become a single economic unit.[7] A wall of protective tariffs would be built up around the Empire and a complicated set of preferences would exist within it.[8] Amery wished to protect British home industries and to favour imports from the colonies over foreign imports. With Britain providing men and money, the Dominions and the Empire would

6. L.S. Amery, *The Forward View* (London, 1935), which is the key work for Amery's systematic thought, p. 112.

7. The authoritative account of Imperial Preference is Julian Amery, *Joseph Chamberlain and the Tariff Reform Campaign* (London, 1969), of which the concluding chapters are especially useful in understanding Leo Amery's ideas over the span of many decades.

8. The British press sometimes put forward the idea of 'Free Trade' within the Empire and Commonwealth, but in fact Amery's plan was an elaborate system of preferences. 'None of the Dominion Governments, as Amery knew only too well, were prepared even to consider Free Trade with Britain. Preference they would give, sometimes by lowering duties in favour of Britain, more often by increasing them against the the foreigner. But nothing would persuade them to dismantle the tariffs protecting their own industries. . . .' Ibid. p. 1020.

provide interdependent markets. With an effective economic and financial framework, the Dominions could work closely together in foreign policy and defence as well as in trade and investment. With a coherent economic system there would develop political and military cooperation. Even before he articulated these ideas systematically as the economic and political programme of Imperial Preference, he inclined in that direction. As a schoolboy he had been impressed with 'what the German *Zollverein* had done to promote German unity'.[9] Since 1834 a German trade area under Prussian auspices had gradually provided the economic basis for political unity. Amery was quick to note that the railway system lay at the heart of Germany's economic strength and that the railways had military ramifications. The example of the German customs union exerted a profound influence on Amery's thought and was the genesis of his advocacy for Imperial Preference, which also had military as well as economic implications.

Amery began his Oxford career at Balliol in 1892 when 'that cherubic, but awe-inspiring figure, Benjamin Jowett' was still Master ('better think before writing next time', was the phrase Amery carried with him as the essence of Jowett's advice).[10] Apart from his pursuit of languages, in which he succeeded brilliantly, his intellectual quest was notable for its concentration on political economy.

9. *My Political Life*, I, p. 52. Amery thus fits well into the context of the late-nineteenth-century debate about economic sources of wealth and Darwinian political evolution as presented in the famous chapter 3 of William L. Langer's *Diplomacy of Imperialism* (New York, 1956 edn.). Two indispensable companions on these and other fundamental issues are Robert J. Scally, *The Origins of the Lloyd George Coalition: The Politics of Social-Imperialism, 1900–1918* (Princeton, 1975); and Paul M. Kennedy, *The Rise of Anglo-German Antagonism 1860–1914* (London, 1980).

10. *My Political Life*, I, p. 47.

One lasting lesson he learned from his Oxford years was the failure of the academic economists to recognize the economic reasons for Bismarck's success, or for that matter the reasons for the emergence of the United States as a world power. 'American *Lebensraum*', in the phrase he used later, was essentially the same as German *Lebensraum* in the sense of a naked reach for economic dominance. From the outset Amery viewed American economic power as a danger to the British Empire. Only if the British organized the resources of the Empire would they be able to survive.[11] On the other hand his political views had not yet crystallized. He called himself a 'Liberal Imperialist' and belonged simultaneously to a Tory club and the Fabian Society. Fabians and forward-looking Tories to his mind had more in common than either had with the Liberals. He was a Unionist, but as much interested in the problems of the Empire as in the politics of the United Kingdom and Ireland or domestic policy. One salient aspect of Amery's political outlook was its consistency. When he arrived at Oxford, he already held the emphatic opinion that Gladstone had given way to the Boers after Majuba and had abandoned Gordon to his fate at Khartoum. 'Gladstone, indeed, then and long afterwards, seemed to me to sum up all that was disastrous in policy and odious in public life.'[12] Amery's earlier views fortified his growing sense of purpose. At Oxford he became a 'professed protectionist' and a 'passionate believer in Empire'. He was now convinced that Imperial Preference was a worthy cause that could be upheld intellectually

11. See G.R. Searle, *The Quest for National Efficiency: A Study in British Politics and Political Thought, 1899–1914* (Berkeley, 1971), which is the essential analysis of this theme.

12. *My Political Life*, I, p. 30.

and morally against the prevailing orthodoxy of Free Trade.

He was elected a Fellow of All Souls College, Oxford, on a second attempt, in 1897, when he was twenty-four years old. The College was a major influence in his formative years and remained important to him until his death in 1955: from the aftermath of the Jameson Raid to the eve of the Suez crisis (had he lived until 1956 would he have seen the comparison with the filibustering expedition of 1896?). These six decades coincided with the golden age of All Souls, which in the early twentieth century captured the public imagination as an intellectual élite with real influence in national and international affairs. Amery wrote in his memoirs: 'Professors, cabinet ministers, bishops, Members of Parliament, civil servants, lawyers, journalists, and business men join [there], on a happy footing of equality.'[13] The 1890s at All Souls was a time of exuberance. 'No one was clamouring to see Queen Victoria Empress of China as well as Empress of India', Amery wrote later. 'But no one . . . would have dismissed the idea as inconceivable.'[14]

Amery was, above all, a man of ideas, not only in a systematic philosophical sense but also as a person keenly interested in history, economics, and public policy.[15] All Souls gave him unrivalled opportunity to test and develop basic arguments and to advance his career in journalism and politics. His introduction to a former Fellow of the

13. Ibid., p. 63.

14. Quoted in Christopher M. Andrew and A.S. Kanya-Forstner, *France Overseas: The Great War and the Climax of French Imperial Expansion* (London, 1981), p. 34—a book of use in this context because of the comparative French perspective.

15. Like J.C. Smuts of South Africa, who became an intimate friend, Amery pursued philosophy throughout his life and planned to publish a book on Spinoza. The manuscript apparently has not survived.

College, G.E. Buckle of *The Times*, he owed to the Warden of All Souls, Sir William Anson, who also put him
up for membership in the Athenaeum in London.[16] The
point about the Athenaeum is significant because of 'contacts', which in a word sums up an important part of
Amery's early life at the College. During his early years
at All Souls he first met Arthur James Balfour, the Prime
Minister. 'I got him into a chair', Amery wrote, 'and like
the Ancient Mariner fixed him with my glittering eye, and
talked at him till four o'clock'—for over three hours,
which is an indication of the young Amery's exuberant
self-confidence.[17] If Amery benefited from such contacts,
he in turn later helped along younger Fellows of All Souls
as he became an indefatigable recruiter for what was
known eventually as 'the establishment'.

He loved the social life and ritual of the College and
once described the Fellows as his 'extended family'. He
was much amused at a comment in the Common Room
by the Professor of Social Anthropology, who said that,
having spent many years among the Bantu, Australian
aborigines, and New Guinea cannibals, he naturally felt

16. Buckle had been a Fellow 1877–85. 'It has occurred to me', Amery
wrote the Warden, '. . . that possibly Mr. Buckle might have some work for
me to do this vacation, either in Austria or Turkey. Could you perhaps make
the suggestion to him?' (Amery to Warden, 10 Dec. 1897, All Souls Archive)
'I have been intending for some time to get myself put up for the Athenaeum
as I believe it takes some 17 years for election. Do you think you could be so
good as to put my name down as a Candidate?' (Amery to Warden, 9 Aug.
1899, ibid.) The Warden gladly complied in these and other of Amery's requests.

17. *Diaries*, I, p. 45. Amery never met Balfour's predecessor, Lord Salisbury, who was a Fellow of the College. But he came to Salisbury's attention.
'Mr. Amery has occupied us a good deal', Salibury wrote to the Warden when
Amery was travelling in the Balkans in 1898. 'It appears . . . to be certain that
he struck a policeman, which in those countries is a grave offence.' (Salisbury
to Anson, 13 Feb. 1898, All Souls Archive) For Amery's account of the incident,
see *My Political Life*, I, pp. 80–83.

at home in the All Souls clan.[18] Among these intellectual cannibals Amery early on began to plan the transformation of the ramshackle Victorian Empire into an economically effective Imperial union. The efficient use of the Empire's resources was a persistent theme in his writings and speeches. He was a driving force in the early stages of the Round Table movement, which aimed to bring about closer unity between Britain and the Dominions.[19] One can trace in his correspondence the vitality of his ideas as they began to clash with Lionel Curtis, who championed a different set of Round Table ideals. Amery aimed first and foremost at economic solidarity, from which he believed political cooperation would naturally develop. Curtis wished to bring about a political federation of the British Empire and Commonwealth that would in turn lead to a world federation—in Amery's view, an illusion. The two remained divided on this fundamental point to the year of both their deaths half a century later.

The contribution of All Souls to Amery's career should not be exaggerated. He created his own opportunities. Yet he regarded the College as a vital part of his mental and moral make-up—in his own words, 'where the world of intellect and that of active life outside come together in the happiest intimacy'.[20] The mystique of All Souls as

18. Amery MS Diary, 6 November 1936. He referred to A.R. Radcliffe-Brown, Fellow of All Souls 1937–46.

19. See Walter Nimocks, *Milner's Young Men: The 'Kindergarten' in Edwardian Imperial Affairs* (Durham, N.C., 1968); and John E. Kendle, *The Round Table Movement and Imperial Union* (Toronto, 1975). David Watt, 'The Men of the Round Table', *Round Table* (July 1969) is a brilliant review of the subject.

20. *My Political Life*, I, p. 55. On this point, see Lord Halifax's speech at Amery's memorial service in *Memorial Addresses of All Souls College Oxford* (Oxford, privately published, 1989).

a powerful influence in British intellectual and political life helped him and others to further their own work and their work in turn perpetuated the mystique. In the public eye the College developed in Amery's time almost an air of mystery about it. There was also a growing public reverence towards it—at least so it seems in retrospect. How much of the image has been burnished by memories of an earlier and more heroic age? In any case the All Souls mystique is not a subject that can easily be assessed. Thus the topic of the shaping of Amery's ideas and the elusive influence of All Souls is problematical. And Amery himself is a figure who puzzles historians. His influence on his contemporaries can easily be detected but is often difficult to judge, just as his notion of All Souls as the spiritual home of the British Empire can be sensed but is hard logically to explain. Therein lies the fascination of the equation of Amery, All Souls, and the British Empire.

Gladstone was an Honorary Fellow of All Souls. Amery never met him, but he relished the College lore about his leisure routine there. Gladstone would read voraciously for long periods of time, interrupting his concentration only for vigorous walks and voluble monologues over tea. As his mind digested massive pieces of information from his reading, he slid unconsciously from one opinion to the next. Amery believed that Gladstonian policy echoed the views most recently heard or read, sometimes, whether consciously or not, for reasons of expediency. He thus explained the turns and shifts of the Liberal Cabinets. By contrast, Amery could never be accused of trimming. But there is a comparison. In a sense, in routine and rectitude, he was as much a Victorian as Mr. Gladstone. Amery's habits were similar. He once clocked his average working day, over a period of a year, at eight hours a day without a break, which meant nine or ten hours most days. And he was exceptionally scrupulous. His closest friend at All Souls at the time, John Simon, who was elected to the College in the same year, cautioned him against going into politics because he was 'too honest'.[21] This was a shrewd comment because Amery's political conscience sometimes prevented him from advancing as quickly as he might have liked. He was a man of undisputed integrity. Churchill described him as 'the straightest man in public life'.[22]

The dominant intellectual and moral influence on Amery throughout his life was Lord Milner. Milner was the older statesman who lent Amery his support and provided him with an example of leadership and courage. To Amery he was an Olympian figure. Milner had spent part of his early life in Germany. He had, like Amery, a slightly European intellect that attached particular value to precision and consistency. Milner had served in Egypt in the early 1890s under Lord Cromer, who described him as 'one of the most able Englishmen who have served the Egyptian government.'[23] In 1897 Milner became High Commissioner in South Africa and soon concluded that Britain and the Boer republics were on collision course. He aimed to unite South Africa under British supremacy. Milner's goals became Amery's goals. Milner inspired not only Amery but other young men of conspicuous ability.[24] Milner's disciples in South Africa became known as the 'Kindergarten' and they in turn became the founders of the Round Table movement. There is an irony in this

21. For Simon and Amery, see David Dutton, *Simon: A Political Biography* (London, 1992), especially pp. 118 and 207.

22. *Diaries*, II, p. 401.

23. Quoted by Basil Williams in the *DNB 1922–1930*, p. 591.

24. For this recurrent theme, see e.g. L.S. Amery, *Thoughts on the Constitution* (Oxford, 1947), p. vii.

because Amery, who was Milner's most ardent follower, never worked directly under him and Milner himself, who inspired the Round Table group, only rarely participated in any of their meetings.

It is worthwhile briefly at this stage to survey the results of Milner's influence on his 'young men' over the longer span because it helps to clarify certain themes about Amery's career. Milner provided the vision, in Amery's words, for people 'who think constructively and Imperially' to galvanize the nation and the Empire.[25] There was an identifiable 'Milner group' at All Souls. It consisted of Amery, Geoffrey (Robinson) Dawson, Dougal Malcolm, Robert Brand, and Lionel Curtis.[26] All had been associated with Milner, some working directly under him and others informally, in the uniting of the South African colonies into a single state. Dawson served as Editor of *The Times* from 1912 to 1919 and again from 1923 to 1941. Malcolm, who had been a member of the Colonial Service, left to join the British South Africa Company in London and eventually rose to its chairmanship and presidency. Brand eventually became Director of Lazard Brothers, the merchant bankers. Curtis did not become a Fellow of All Souls until 1921, but he had been the Beit Lecturer in Colonial History in 1912 and until the early part of the First World War devoted himself to the study of federation within the British Commonwealth.[27] Curtis was the guiding spirit behind the Round Table movement—in Amery's

25. Amery to Milner, 26 February 1904, Amery Papers.

26. Geoffrey Dawson changed his name from Robinson to Dawson in 1917. Here he is Dawson throughout.

27. See Lionel Curtis, *The Problem of the Commonwealth* (London, 1916), and *The Commonwealth of Nations* (London, 1916). On Curtis, see especially Deborah Lavin, 'Lionel Curtis and the Idea of Commonwealth', in Frederick Madden and D.K. Fieldhouse, eds., *Oxford and the Idea of Commonwealth* (London, 1982).

words, the 'indefatigable peripatetic prophet and mission-ary' of closer union and federation.[28]

When Milner's disciples returned to England in the dec-ade after the Boer War they frequently met, with others, in London formally to establish the Round Table move-ment. The broader membership included F.S. Oliver, who was a businessman and man of letters.[29] In 1906 Oliver published a biography of *Alexander Hamilton*, which at the time was widely regarded as a brilliant interpretation of the federal principles of the U.S. Constitution as well as an incisive study of Hamilton's character. The Hamilton biography served as a guide to the men working for the further union of South Africa and later for the federation of the British Commonwealth. In Amery's view, however, American federalism was a false example for the evolution of the Empire, but Oliver's work captured Curtis's imag-ination and Amery cherished his friendship. Two other friends should be mentioned here because they became close associates. These are Philip Kerr (Lord Lothian), who served as Lloyd George's Private Secretary during the latter part of the First World War and, later, as Am-bassador to the United States 1939–1940; and Edward Grigg, who became Governor of Kenya during Amery's tenure as Colonial Secretary and, eventually, Minister Res-ident in the Middle East during the last part of the Second

---

28. *My Political Life*, I, p. 270.

29. 'He wrote English prose with the clear precision of Swift.' (Dougal Malcolm in the *Dictionary of National Biography 1931–1940*). Oliver's books included *Federalism and Home Rule* (London, 1910), *The Alternatives to Civil War* (London, 1913), and his most famous work, *The Endless Adventure* (2 vols., London, 1930–31), which is a study of the art of politics. Following Oliver's inspiration, Amery wrote in his Chichele Lectures of 1947 that politics was 'a never-ending adventure' and that 'one remains content to believe that the game itself was good, and that one played one's best for one's own chosen goals, and by one's own rules.' *Thoughts on the Constitution*, pp. vii–viii.

World War. In 1910 Kerr became the first editor of the *Round Table*, the journal established to promote the aims of the movement. Grigg joined him in 1913 as joint editor. Amery's stalwart friendship with these men, despite occasional differences, provides an important clue to the secrets, successes, and frustrations of his life.

Milner's influence on Amery, and the early controversies between Amery and Curtis about the *Round Table*, brought about a crystallization of principle on the part of Amery which retained a bedrock quality during the rest of his career.[30] At the time of the founding of the journal, there were heated debates about purpose and tactics. Amery and Curtis held opposite views on a central point. Curtis believed that the Dominions should be convinced that the British Empire would break up unless they agreed to an act of union or federation. 'His passionate sincerity and energy, as well as the indisputable logic of his arguments,' Amery wrote later, 'tended to dominate our councils.'[31] Still, Amery held to the contrary. 'What we want', he wrote at the time, 'is in fact not a brand new constitution, but an effective reorganization of the constitution which we already possess.' He believed it would be 'constitutional hara-kiri' to sacrifice the continuity of the British system for an artificial union on the American principle.[32] He never wavered in the belief that it was a mistake to place before the Dominions the 'false dilemma' of break-up or federation.

30. Nevertheless Milner chiseled away at Amery's dogmatism, especially on the issue of Imperial Preference.'I have always been somewhat uneasy', he wrote to Amery, 'about the too exclusive attention paid to Tariff Reform, and the exaggerated language used about it'. Milner to Amery, 28 January 1913, Amery Papers.

31. *My Political Life*, I, p. 348.

32. For recent assessment of Amery's constitutional judgement, see Ferdinand Mount, *The British Constitution Now* (London, 1992), p. 179.

Amery acknowledged the insight of Richard Jebb, the economist and publicist, who refused to join the Round Table group precisely because he thought they were perverting the proper development of the Empire. Jebb saw earlier than anyone else that the Dominions would develop their own sense of national identity which might, or might not, conflict with allegiance to the Commonwealth.[33] Like Jebb, Amery had a pragmatic turn of mind. He was interested in practical measures that would bring about closer economic union, which he regarded, in his phrase, as 'the master key to the whole problem'. He gradually drifted away from the inner circle of the Round Table movement. In retrospect it is clear that Amery and Jebb had a more perceptive understanding of nationalism in the white Dominions than did Curtis. Self-governing communities overseas could not be made or persuaded to federate. Amery never favoured the 'either—or' 'federate or break up' argument. Sir Keith Hancock in his biography of J.C. Smuts of South Africa pays supreme tribute to Amery by stating that his early opposition to Imperial Federation destined him in his later political career 'to render signal service to the cause of sovereign equality and national freedom in the Dominions and India.'[34]

* * *

It is useful to see the main contours of Amery's career in relation to his original motivation. In a letter to John Simon at All Souls in 1897, Amery described 'the [British] Imperialist running the whole world on sound economic

33. For Jebb, see J.D.B. Miller, *Richard Jebb and the Problem of Empire* (London, 1956), and the seminal work edited by John Eddy and Deryck Schreuder, *The Rise of Colonial Nationalism* (Sydney, 1988).

34. W.K. Hancock, *Smuts* (2 vols., London, 1962 and 1968), I, p. 459.

and self-government principles.'[35] In 1899–1902 he put his theories to the test against the background of the Boer War. During this period he worked as a war correspondent for *The Times*. He continued with the newspaper until 1909 as a leader writer and as the editor and principal author of the seven-volume exhaustive account of the conflict, *The Times History of the War in South Africa*.[36] In 1911 he was elected Conservative Member of Parliament for South Birmingham (Sparkbrook), a seat he held for thirty-four years until the Labour landslide in 1945. In the pre-First World War period, some of the principal themes of his career were the advocacy for military reform, the development of his economic ideas, and the shaping of his geo-political views.

When Amery arrived in South Africa in September 1899, shortly before the outbreak of the war, he met J.C. Smuts, who was to become South Africa's Prime Minister as well as Amery's lifelong friend and intellectual companion. Amery immediately formed a high estimate of the Boer adversaries. 'They are all very confident of victory, especially the real Boer,' he wrote, 'who I can picture to you best as a Swiss guide on horseback with a rifle over his shoulder instead of rope and axe.'[37] To his dismay he found the British Army almost a complete contrast. 'The incapacity, indecision and timidity displayed by our Commanding Officers is something awful', he reported to the Foreign Editor of *The Times*, Sir Valentine Chirol.[38] Much

35. Amery to Simon, 20 March 1897, Simon Papers 47.

36. L.S. Amery, ed., *The Times History of the War in South Africa, 1899–1902* (7 vols., London, 1900–09). For Amery within the general context of British journalism, see Stephen Koss, *The Rise and Fall of the Political Press in Britain. Vol. II: The Twentieth Century* (Chapel Hill, N.C., 1984).

37. *Diaries*, I, p. 30.

38. Ibid.

of Amery's writing as war correspondent appeared anonymously, which in his own view was just as well because otherwise he would have been dismissed, in his phrase, as a whipper-snapper.[39] 'Antiquated stupidity' were the words he used to describe the mentality of the British officers. He became uncomfortably aware that Australians serving in South Africa were contemptuous of their British comrades-in-arms. Yet the 'caste system' of the British Army relegated the 'colonials' to inferior military and social positions. Amery became a powerful defender of the proposition that Australians were political allies who should be allowed to rise to the level of the British Cabinet. Unlike Churchill, he did not view them as second-class citizens. Amery's service as war correspondent thus prepared him for some of the actual developments of the First World War (including Dominion participation in the Imperial War Cabinet). Most important of all, he received a military education on the battlefields of South Africa.

In his published despatches as well as in his private letters, he championed the cause of Milner, who described himself in the South African context as elsewhere as an 'Imperialist out and out'. It is important to grasp Milner's vision of the future of South Africa because Amery embraced it so wholeheartedly. Milner believed that all of South Africa should constitute '*one Dominion*', as he emphasized it himself, 'with a common government dealing with Customs, Railways, and Defence, perhaps also with Native policy.' The black African populations would play a subordinate part in South African society for the indefinite future, perhaps even for centuries, and they would

---

39. He synthesized his ideas under his own name in *The Problem of the Army* (London, 1903). For discussion of his lessons drawn from the Boer War, see Searle, *The Quest for National Efficiency*, chap. 2.

have to be ruled with a firm and even hand. On this point both Milner and Amery shared racial views that were characteristic of their era. 'The *ultimate* end', Milner wrote, 'is a self-governing white Community, supported by *well-treated* and *justly governed* black labour from Cape Town to Zambesi.'[40] Amery's contemporary views were identical, though more crudely expressed. 'South Africa must develop as a white man's country under the guidance of white men, and not as a bastard country like most of South America.'[41]

Milner believed that the Afrikaners could live harmoniously with the British on the model of the French- and English-speaking peoples of Canada. 'First beaten, then fairly treated', he wrote of the archetypal Boer, ' . . . I think he will be peaceful enough.'[42] Milner's ideas bore similarity to those of Lord Durham in 1839 for the elimination of French-Canadian nationalism. The long hand of Durham, indeed, stretched not only to Milner's reconstruction in South Africa but, later, to Amery's policy in India. Amery identified himself with Durham in the tra-

40. Cecil Headlam, ed., *The Milner Papers 1897–1905* (2 vols., 1931–33), II, p. 35. The best analysis of Milner's thought on these points is by L.M. Thompson, *The Unification of South Africa 1902–1910* (Oxford, 1960), chap. 1.

41. 'In five hundred years' time I expect the South African white man will contain a strong dark blend, and the end of all things may be a brown South African race, comparable to the Abyssinians or Somalis. That doesn't matter, what does matter is that there should not be too quick a mixture now or for the next few centuries.' He also wrote in the same letter: 'We have done one good thing towards conciliating the Dutch: that is, we have shown our resolve not to let the natives get out of bounds.' (Amery to Chirol, 7 July 1900, *Diaries*, I, pp. 36–37) For the context of Amery's racial assumptions, see Michael Howard, 'Empire, Race and War in pre-1914 Britain', in Hugh Lloyd-Jones and others, eds., *History and Imagination* (London, 1981). See also David E. Omissi, *Air Power and Colonial Control* (Manchester, 1990), p. 110. For Amery and the theme of eugenics, see Paul B. Rich, *Race and Empire in British Politics* (Cambridge, 1986).

42. Headlam, *Milner Papers*, II, p. 36.

dition of constitutional reform as an instrument of progress. In the same vein, Milner articulated for South Africa the central proposition of granting freedom in order to preserve Imperial control. He wrote of the two Afrikaner states then being subjected to British rule: 'I believe in a lot of *virtual self-government* in the new Colonies, without letting the supreme control out of Imperial hands.' He favoured the development of strong federal government, but with continued British control over finance, defence, the police. Self-government, or 'responsible government', should not be granted until it would perpetuate the same purpose as that of the Imperial government. 'We must be very sure of our ground', Milner wrote, 'before we part with executive authority . . . we shall always keep Imperial control . . . till we can with safety grant "responsible government" to a Federated South Africa.'[43]

Amery's sentiments were identical. 'There can be no talk of a *Dominion* for *years* and *years* after the annexation', he reported to Chirol at *The Times* after a conversation with Milner, 'not until you have a large English majority in the Transvaal and a fair-sized English population in Rhodesia.'[44] When he later grappled with the problem of the transfer of power in India, there was of course no question of trying to determine the future by strength of British numbers; but the lesson he had learned from South Africa on the timing and the delicacy of withdrawing executive authority was, he believed, exactly the same. He became committed to a free and independent India within the Commonwealth; but until the Indians themselves could agree on a constitution, the British would retain control over the vital areas of finance, de-

43. Ibid., p. 244.
44. Amery to Chirol, 25 October 1899, *Diaries*, I, p. 30.

fence, and foreign policy. In South Africa in 1906 and in India in 1947 the timetable was accelerated to preserve goodwill; in both cases Amery believed that the calculated risk of 'magnanimity' paid off.

His economic thought interlocked with Milner's idea that material progress would promote political unity. Milner planned to develop the gold-mining industry of the Witwatersrand and to modernize agricultural and stock-raising techniques in South Africa. His policy could be summed up in the two words, 'lift' and 'overspill'. By the latter term he meant the surplus of revenue that would come from an expanded mining industry and would be used to lift the standards of living of the two new colonies to a higher level.[45] Extra income would also be used to finance massive immigration of British settlers, who would numerically swamp the Boers and achieve the political end of ensuring British supremacy. Such measures would transform South Africa from 'the weakest link in the imperial chain' into one of the linchpins of the Empire. The concept of political and strategic strength flowing from economic development fired Amery's imagination. Here he proved to be far more supple and resourceful than Milner, whose mind in some respects was more rigid and doctrinaire. One of the lasting lessons that Amery learned from the Boer War was that enduring political arrangements cannot be forced on an unwilling people. First build the economic links, then reconstruct the political relationship—this sequence of action became Amery's governing precept in his crusade for Imperial Preference. Nevertheless, from the perspective of the Afrikaners it must have seemed odd that the proposition of 'equality'

45. *My Political Life*, I, p. 174.

marched hand in hand with the assumption that the Transvaal would become thoroughly British.[46] On the British side itself there was a flaw in the plan. British immigrants proved unwilling to settle in the Transvaal. There were only seven hundred British families in 1906 despite a subsidy of £2,200,000. 'I do not think it is very encouraging that we should have spent so much money upon the settlement of so few', Churchill commented at the time.[47]

Amery was in every sense Milner's political disciple. Milner had clarity of mind and strength of will. His general ideas stimulated Amery as they did the other young men of the Round Table movement, but more specifically Milner's sense of a just cause inspired his followers. Milner held that the purpose of the struggle in South Africa was not British hegemony but the equality of the British and the Afrikaners. How can Amery's unreserved endorsement of this proposition be explained? With the benefit of hindsight on the Afrikaner response to the grand design planned by Milner and embraced by Amery, it is fair to ask whether there was an element of self-deception. How did Amery in retrospect see the causes and consequences of the Boer War? One answer is that he never wavered in his view. Throughout his life he believed that the aims were noble, the cause just. He wrote of Milner in 1953 in a passage uninhibited by critical judgement:

46. As a corrective to Amery's optimistic assessment of 'equality' rather than 'hegemony', see Donald Denoon, *A Grand Illusion: The Failure of Imperial Policy in the Transvaal Colony During the Period of Reconstruction 1900–1905* (London, 1973). See also Kent Fedorowich, 'Anglicization and the Politicization of British Immigration to South Africa, 1899–1929', *Journal of Imperial and Commonwealth History*, XIX, 2 (May 1991), esp. p. 229.

47. Quoted by Ronald Hyam, *Historical Journal*, XII (1969), p. 173. For Amery's projects on 'Empire Settlement' (a theme I have not pursued here), see Stephen Constantine, ed., *Emigrants and Empire* (Manchester, 1990).

His imperialism was the radical imperialism . . . of free and equal partnership in the Commonwealth. It was for that principle, and not for that of United Kingdom domination, that he faced, and forced, the issue of equal rights of English and Afrikaner in South Africa. It was for that end that he carried out his great work of reconstruction in the conquered Republics.[48]

Amery had no sympathy for the brand of radicalism espoused by the 'pro-Boers' and 'Little Englanders' who believed that the war was a mistake. To balance Amery's staunch defence of Milner, it is appropriate to quote the historian Max Beloff, who has written in *Imperial Sunset*: 'Whatever the historian may now see as being the primary cause of the conflict, to many people at the time the case against Britain seemed an overwhelming one. Here was a great empire fighting to destroy the independence of two small pastoral republics for the sake of the profits of mineowners and financiers.'[49]

Amery's strength was his sense of purpose, which permeated his own contemporary account. The Liberal historian H.A.L. Fisher wrote in a review: 'in his hands *The Times History of the War* is a history with a mission. Its aim is to defend Imperialism in the past, to make Imperialists in the present, and, by displaying not only the virtues but also the faults of British organization to strengthen the Empire against the perils of the future.'[50] Amery did not finish the history until 1909.[51] He calculated

48. *My Political Life*, II, p. 211.

49. Max Beloff, *Imperial Sunset* (2 vols., London, 1969 and 1989), I, p. 78.

50. *My Political Life*, I, p. 336.

51. Amery encountered difficulties with the staff of *The Times* because of the length and the protracted time it took to write the account. On one occasion he told Moberly Bell, the manager of the paper, that a wounded officer had the *History* read to him by his wife. The quick-witted Bell responded with a notice recording the officer's death 'after long sufferings heroically endured'. *Diaries*, I, p. 37.

that it took him the equivalent of five years of his working life. Because of the commitment to *The Times* he could not accept an offer made by Milner to become his secretary, which probably would have led to significant administrative responsibilities after the close of the war. Amery thus remained, in his own phrase, an 'honorary member' of the Milner 'Kindergarten' of Oxford men taking part in the reconstruction of the Transvaal. He probably provided Milner with an incomparably more valuable service by acting as his spokesman in the anonymous editorials of *The Times*. Amery's efforts were prodigious, sometimes producing as many as three leaders in one edition.

The first of the future Kindergarten to arrive in South Africa was Peter Perry, who had defeated Amery in his first bid for an All Souls Fellowship in 1896. 'I have severe accesses of nostalgia for the common room of All Souls from time to time', Perry wrote in 1901 to Geoffrey Dawson, who was then at the Colonial Office. 'It will be bitter to think you are gathering in hall making salad, & flocking round the Warden as he stands with his back to the fireplace.'[52] Such details would not be remarkable but for the mutual bond of All Souls that later made it one of the natural meeting places when the members of the Kindergarten became the founders of the Round Table movement. Amery once participated in a miniature All Souls Gaudy, or College reunion, in Johannesburg with Perry, Dawson, and Robert Brand.[53] The exuberance of such occasions made it easy for them to think, in the words of a later satire of All Souls, that the College was 'an unof-

52. Quoted in Nimocks, *Milner's Young Men*, p. 52.
53. *My Political Life*, I, p. 321.

ficial committee for running . . . the destinies of the British Empire.'[54]

At the close of the Boer War, Amery returned to England. In 1903 Joseph Chamberlain resigned from the Cabinet to appeal to the nation to look to the future of the Empire, to develop its vast territories, and to reform the existing fiscal system.[55] He attempted to establish as a national goal the aim that had already become Amery's life's work. Amery now threw himself heart and soul into the campaign. Using the pseudonym 'Tariff Reformer' in *The Times*, he attacked the doctrinaire assumption of the Free Traders ('I did not wish my attack to be side-tracked', he wrote, 'by questions as to who was this young man, not yet in his thirties, who poured contempt on all the greatest economists of the age.')[56] He published a polemic, a book entitled *The Fundamental Fallacies of Free Trade.*[57] He now became an ardent spokesman for Chamberlain's economic programme of Imperial Preference.

It is important to be clear about the nature of the economic system advocated by Chamberlain and Amery and to pursue its implications. In substance it was a sophisticated version of the old mercantilist system whereby Britain would become the workshop of the colonies which in turn would provide markets and raw materials.[58] The Brit-

54. Anon. (C.W. Brodribb, a staff member of *The Times* under Dawson), *Government by Mallardry: A Study in Political Ornithology* (London, 1932); copy in the Codrington Library, All Souls College; see also Dawson Papers, Box 80.

55. See Julian Amery, *Joseph Chamberlain and the Tariff Reform Campaign*.

56. *My Political Life*, I, p. 246.

57. L.S. Amery, *The Fundamental Fallacies of Free Trade* (London, 1906).

58. The most trenchant analysis of Chamberlain's economics is by W.K. Hancock, *Survey of British Commonwealth Affairs: Problems of Nationality, 1918–1936*, (Oxford, 1937), pp. 39ff. See also D.K. Fieldhouse, *Economics and Empire* (London, 1973), pp. 328–29; and Ian M. Drummond, *British Economic Policy and the Empire* (London, 1972), pp. 40–42. The best account of Amery's economic ideas is the editorial comment in the Amery *Diaries*, II, *passim*.

ish Empire would emerge as a single and prosperous economic unit with an unbroken tariff wall around it, which in turn would enhance British power throughout the world. Prosperity within the Empire would improve conditions within the United Kingdom. Imperial strength would guarantee British security against Germany and the United States. 'Joseph Chamberlain was concerned first and last', Amery once wrote, 'with Britain's position in the world, with Imperial unity and with social welfare.'[59] Interpreted in a different way, as it was for example in Germany and the United States, the co-ordinated development and concerted political and military strength of the British Empire would make Britain, perhaps, the dominant power in the world. Such was the implicit *realpolitik*.

Power is a relative concept. In the decade before 1914 Amery began to fear the relative decline of Britain as the leading industrial and commercial power in view of the corresponding rise of Germany.[60] When he first made an unsuccessful bid for a Parliamentary seat in 1906, he explained to the voters of Wolverhampton East:

Every year the competition for power among the great world states is getting keener, and unless we can continue to hold our own, unless we can keep our invincible Navy, and unless we can defend the Empire at every one of its frontiers, our Empire and our trade will be taken away from us by others and we shall be starved out, invaded, trampled under foot and utterly ruined.

But how can these little islands hold their own in the

59. *My Political Life*, III, p. 225.

60. For Amery's ideas in this context, see especially Zara S. Steiner, *Britain and the Origins of the First World War* (London, 1977), p. 67 *et passim*.

long run against such great and rich Empires as the United States and Germany are rapidly becoming, or even as Russia will be when it recovers from its present [1905] disasters?

How can we with our forty millions of people compete against states nearly double our size?[61]

Even if the resources of the Empire were efficiently utilized, could Britain hold her own?

As Amery answered those questions, he drew on an idea from a lecture he had attended at the Royal Geographical Society in 1904 by Halford Mackinder entitled 'The Geographical Pivot of History.'[62] Mackinder developed the theme of a 'correlation' between geography, economic strength, and military power. Germany occupied the heart of the European continent. By industrial growth, and specifically by railway construction, she threatened to become the dominant military power. Amery adjusted the proposition to British circumstances. British supremacy could be revived or sustained by developing the industrial potential of Britain and the agricultural wealth of the colonies, by building British railways in Africa and Asia, and by modernizing the Royal Navy. It was an almost intoxicating vision. The British Empire extended over one fourth of the world. In the phrase that he eventually used frequently, 'the Southern British world' would provide both military and economic strength. At the 1904 meeting at the Royal Geographical Society, Amery began the discussion by adding his own corollary to Mackinder's theory

61. Quoted in Kennedy, *The Rise of the Anglo-German Antagonism*, pp. 307–08.

62. *Geographical Journal*, XXIII (April 1904).

of the heartland.[63] Air power combined with sea power might redress the balance against European rivals. Here was one of the axioms of Amery's strategic thought, articulated only a few months after the flight of the Wright brothers at Kitty Hawk.[64]

Amery's interest in grand strategy and the Empire bore fruit at All Souls. In the early twentieth century, neither military nor colonial history was taught at Oxford. Amery persuaded All Souls to establish an endowment for a readership in military history in 1905.[65] It finds its present-day incarnation in the Chichele Professorship in the History of War. He was also responsible for the Beit endowment for the history of the British Empire, today the Beit Professorship in the History of the British Commonwealth. At a dinner in London in 1904, he met Alfred Beit, the South African diamond magnate and admirer of Rhodes. This was the year of the creation of the Rhodes Scholarships. Amery remarked that it was absurd that the Rhodes Scholars would come to the 'heart of the Empire' only to find that no one taught colonial history. Beit replied that something must be done. What? 'A professor of Colonial History at £900 a year' responded Amery. Beit agreed even before they had finished the soup.[66] Amery

63. L.S. Amery, 'Discussion following the presentation of "The Geographical Pivot of History" by H.J. Mackinder', *Geographical Journal*, XXIII (April 1904). For discussion of Amery and other geo-political theorists of the early twentieth century, see Paul M. Kennedy, *The Rise and Fall of British Naval Mastery* (London, 1976), esp. p. 184. For the naval dimension of Amery's thought, see also Rhodri Williams, *Defending the Empire: The Conservative Party and British Defence Policy 1899–1915* (London, 1991), p. 198.

64. See Geoffrey Parker, *Western Geopolitical Thought in the Twentieth Century* (London, 1985), pp. 32–33.

65. *My Political Life*, I, pp. 221.

66. Ibid., pp. 184–85. Beit also agreed to provide for assistants or lecturers as well as for books and prizes. Lionel Curtis, as has been seen, was one of the early beneficiaries.

took the next train to Oxford. All Souls became the seat of colonial history until the end of the tenure of Sir Reginald Coupland, who was a Fellow of the College until 1948 (when the Chair was moved to Balliol). Amery served as one of Coupland's electors in 1920.[67] Coupland himself became a foremost member of the Round Table movement and influenced Amery's ideas, especially on Palestine and India.

Before the First World War Amery also took part in an intellectual society in London called the 'Coefficients'. The organizers were Sidney and Beatrice Webb. The members included Bertrand Russell, Mackinder, H.G. Wells, W.A.S. Hewins (a tariff reformer and Director of the London School of Economics), Julian Corbett (the naval historian), Charles à Court Repington (the military critic), and W.F. Monypenny (then writing the life of Disraeli).[68] One of the purposes of this 'Brains Trust', as Amery later called it, was to address squarely the problem of national decline and how to reverse it. In the novel *The New Machiavelli*, H.G. Wells satirically depicted Amery as 'Crupp', one of the prominent members. Crupp suffered from a recurrent nightmare of the British Empire as a 'Brontosaurus' with its backbone bigger than its cranium.[69] It was a telling remark. Throughout Amery's writ-

67. 'You will remember', Coupland wrote to Amery in a pensive mood in 1939, 'that you were one of the electors who appointed me to the Beit Chair nearly twenty years ago.' (Coupland to Amery, 2 Jan. 1939, Papers of the Rhodes Trust 2698.) Amery thus helped to make an appointment at the seminal stage in the development of the history of the British Empire as an academic subject.

68. Amery was also the founder of a club of young Tories called the 'Compatriots', a more directly Chamberlainite group. Both groups are discussed in *My Political Life*, I, chaps. IX and X. For analysis of the politics of the Coefficients and Compatriots as well as the larger issues involved, see Scally, *Origins of the Lloyd George Coalition*, chaps. 3 and 4.

69. H.G. Wells, *The New Machiavelli* (New York, 1910), p. 329.

ing on army reform, economics, and geo-politics, he aimed to transform the antediluvian British Empire of the nineteenth century into a modern version with brains as well as backbone.

The theme of Amery and the Empire in the pre-First World War period must also be seen in relation to his career in journalism and politics. His book published in 1903, *The Problem of the Army*, established his reputation as a military reformer by relentlessly arguing the need for a high-quality Regular Army.[70] His mind was working in the same direction as those within the government in the Committee of Imperial Defence. Three years later, in 1906, some of his critics regarded *Fundamental Fallacies of Free Trade* as economic heresy. But it argued a strong case for Imperial Preference and set the mould for his economic thought for some fifty years. Above all, in the realm of journalism his success was spectacular because Lord Northcliffe offered him the editorship of the *Observer* in 1908 and wished him to succeed Buckle at *The Times* in 1912. Amery successfully supported Geoffrey Dawson as the candidate for *The Times* position, but in 1911 Amery himself had at last won a seat in the House of Commons. In pursuing his political career he carried forward the crusade of Joseph Chamberlain. It was Neville Chamberlain who made possible the Birmingham constituency for him.[71]

There is one part of Amery's life before the war that also needs to be emphasized because otherwise the intel-

70. But, for the point of view that he was merely a 'military gadfly', see Nicholas d'Ombrain, *War Machinery and High Policy: Defence Administration in Peacetime Britain 1902–1914* (Oxford, 1973), p. 174.

71. 'I owe it nearly all to Neville Chamberlain', Amery wrote in April 1911. *Diaries*, I, p. 78. See David Dilks, *Neville Chamberlain: Pioneering and Reform, 1869–1929* (Cambridge, 1984), p. 123.

lectual dynamo of efficiency and precision cannot be understood in human terms. In 1910 he married Florence ('Bryddie' or 'B.') Greenwood, who was of Canadian origin and the sister of Hamar (Lord) Greenwood, who was already a Member of Parliament. This was a happy marriage from which Amery drew much inner strength. Milner wrote to Bryddie shortly before the marriage: 'I have a very genuine affection and admiration for him as a man —for his strength, his simplicity, his kindliness, his utter lack of vanity or pettiness.'[72]

At about the time of his marriage and his election to Parliament, Amery became engrossed in the Irish problem. So strong was the preoccupation with the drift towards civil war that one is reminded of the theme of George Dangerfield's book, *The Strange Death of Liberal England*, in which the coincidental outbreak of the European war deflected a British revolution.[73] Amery himself reflected in his memoirs that 'we seemed perilously near to civil war before greater events outside averted that calamity.'[74] He was a passionate opponent of Home Rule. With remarkable logic that he would later apply to Palestine and Pakistan, he asked the basic question, 'what is a nation?' To him the United Kingdom was a great and unified nation composed of Scots, Welsh, and Irish, but a tyranny of an Irish minority could not be allowed to dictate the

72. *Diaries*, I, p. 71. Milner also wrote: 'This is between ourselves. I don't want even Leo to see this letter which is written from the bottom of my heart.' (Milner to Miss Greenwood, 27 Oct. 1910)

73. Dangerfield's classic work is of interest here because, despite the similarity of theme, he wrote from the opposite vantage point of Amery and attacked the idea of 'Imperial England, beribboned and bestarred and splendid, living in majestic profusion up till the very moment of war.' *The Strange Death of Liberal England* (New York, 1935), p. 394. See also especially Patricia Jallard, *The Liberals and Ireland: The Ulster Question in British Politics to 1914* (Brighton, 1980).

74. *My Political Life*, I, p. 435.

fate of the overall British majority or to inflict its will on another minority, the people of Ulster. He concluded that there were 'two nations' in Ireland in much the same way that he later argued that there were two nations in India. Taking into account the Scots, Amery made a case for the self-determination of the *British* people. He stated in one of his early speeches in the House of Commons:

> Let us understand what we mean by the word 'nation'. If we only mean a moral unity, a community of ideals, of traditions, of manner, of literature, such a unit as Scotland is to-day in its utmost vigour and highest perfection, then in that sense there is not one of us who would not help Ireland to be a nation.

Ireland was, however, entirely different from Scotland:

> [U]nfortunately Ireland is not a nation in that [Scottish] sense. Hon. Members who plead so eloquently for Irish nationality have made little effort to reconcile the two nations at present in Ireland. You certainly cannot reconcile them by handing over the smaller nation to the servitude of the larger.[75]

Amery never quite reconciled the logic of self-determination in the Irish case in the way in which he did later with the cases of Pakistan and Israel, when he eventually accepted the claims of small nations and indeed championed the cause of national independence. In studying his speeches and his diary entries on Ireland, it is hard not to conclude that he was a captive of some of the political and racial ideas of his time, some of which make disagreeable reading today. 'They are a solid determined looking

75. *Parliamentary Debates* (Commons), 30 April 1912, col. 1786.

lot these Ulstermen', Amery wrote to 'B.' in 1912,'—no more Irish than they are Chinese and with not much more use for "Papishes" than they have for "Chinks" or niggers.'[76]

In the summer of 1914 Amery accepted the plunge into European war as an inevitable event long in the making. There was no doubt in his mind that German militarism was the underlying cause. At the time and forever after he argued that the Kaiser and his Prussian advisers made a fundamental error in assessing the nature of the British Empire:

> Looked at through German spectacles the British Empire had long appeared to be in process of disintegration. It seemed natural to expect that the moment of England's entanglement in a great war would give the signal for armed revolt in India and South Africa, as well as in Ireland, and for an attitude of increasing detachment by the other Dominions.[77]

If there happened to be something inevitable about the conflict between Britain and Germany, there was nothing inevitable that the Liberal government—especially one that included Sir Edward Grey as Foreign Secretary— would respond vigorously and decisively. As a young and junior Member of Parliament, Amery played an important part in stiffening the attitude of the government by helping to persuade the Tory leadership, especially Lord Lansdowne, that the nation should resolutely and courageously enter the war. Had it not been for Tory insistence on a decisive course, in Amery's view, the Liberal government

76. *Diaries*, I, p. 84.
77. *My Political Life*, II, p. 15.

might have wobbled in the same way that Gladstone had proved to be indecisive earlier. Amery found Grey's famous speech on the declaration of war so boring in its hesitation and lack of clear purpose that he actually fell asleep in the midst of it. In Amery's opinion it would have been far better to have declared war unequivocally and boldly. In the end, Amery reflected, the Liberal government, with Tory prodding, managed to strike the right chord: 'we went into the war as a united nation and remained united through undreamt of efforts and sacrifices of blood and treasure. We fought it as a united Commonwealth and Empire, and in the course of it achieved a greater measure of effective Imperial unity in its direction than statesmanship had ever contemplated before, or has achieved since.'[78]

* * *

During the early part of the First World War, Amery served as an intelligence officer in Flanders, the Balkans, Gallipoli, and Salonika. This was a period of frustration in his career. He hoped to serve in a capacity that would make full use of his talents, but he was rebuffed. He witnessed the 'inefficiency' and 'incompetence' of the Asquith government waging war. The Prime Minister—'Squiff', in the irreverent phrase used by Amery and others—distrusted Amery because of his close contacts with the right-wing press and military officers such as General Sir Henry Wilson, who eventually became Chief of the Imperial General Staff. Amery felt an affinity to Wilson, who was also a Unionist and a Milnerite. Lloyd George knew of these political connections and once commented on Mil-

78. Ibid., p. 32.

ner's influence with 'the Tory intelligentsia' and the generals.[79] Wilson possessed a free-booting, conspiratorial intellect. Like Amery, he regarded Milner as one of the few British politicians who possessed the discipline and drive to bring the war to a successful conclusion. The following excerpt from a note from Wilson to Amery conveys the exasperation at the lack of direction of the Asquith regime as well as the underlying intrigue of the Milnerites:

18.12.15

My dear Leo,

I saw Milner yesterday. The outlook is certainly not bright, & the darkest part is the difficulty of getting rid of Squiff. And yet it *must* be done if we are to win the war. We can't win if we have to carry him. . . .

Henry[80]

Milner himself during this period pressed for Amery's appointment to a suitable position. His knowledge of war, Milner wrote, '& of foreign countries, ideas & *languages*, far exceeds that of any man of his age that I know.'[81]

When Lloyd George came to power in December 1916, Milner became a member of the War Cabinet. At Milner's

79. See A.J.P. Taylor, *English History 1914–1945* (Oxford, 1965), p. 75, n. 1.

80. Amery Papers. A.M. Gollin, *Proconsul in Politics: A Study of Lord Milner in Opposition and in Power* (London, 1964), p. 322. Gollin notes that Wilson was, perhaps, 'the most accomplished intriguer produced by the British Army in recent times.' (p. 243) According to Amery: 'It was not till Milner became Secretary of State for War in 1918 and Henry Wilson Chief of Staff that Lloyd George could reckon upon either the ability or the whole-hearted co-operation of the War Office, or the War Office feel that its views carried real weight with the Prime Minister.' *My Political Life*, II, p. 97.

81. Milner to Austen Chamberlain, 20 May 1915, Bonar Law Papers 50/3/9.

insistence, Amery was appointed to the Secretariat, which played a critical part in the overall direction of the war effort.[82] For the Milner group it was the outcome of a long and difficult struggle for ascendancy. Amery had provided Milner with plans and advice at every step of the way. Amery and Dawson had helped to bring Milner and Lloyd George into alliance. In their own minds, the Milnerites regarded themselves as having a strength of purpose necessary for the great national emergency, but to others their collaboration smacked of conspiracy. Sir Maurice Hankey was Amery's immediate superior in the War Cabinet Secretariat.[83] He was well aware, in his own words, that Amery was 'the very soul of the . . . horrible intrigues against the [Asquith] government'. Hankey may be pardoned for having, at least at first, a negative impression of Amery: 'He is a scheming little devil . . .'[84] In his memoirs Amery referred to Hankey merely as a man with a 'clear head and practical ability'. Hankey did impart to him one bureaucratic principle of supreme value: however woolly the discussion of a Cabinet or a committee, the Secretary must provide a conclusion. Amery found that if he invented a good conclusion it was rarely queried.[85]

Amery once described the War Cabinet as a 'Committee

82. For an analysis of the politics of this body, see John Turner, *Lloyd George's Secretariat* (Cambridge, 1980); more generally, the same author's invaluable *British Politics and the Great War* (London, 1992).

83. Hankey acquiesced in the appointment, 'as Lord Milner insists . . . though I always suspect him [Amery] of being anti-Russian, and would much rather see him elsewhere.' (Hankey to Lloyd George, 14 Dec. 1916, Lloyd George Papers (F/23/1/2).

84. Stephen Roskill, *Hankey: Man of Secrets* (2 vols., London, 1970 and 1972), I, pp. 270 and 353. The Assistant Secretary to the War Cabinet, Thomas Jones, also at first found Amery an unattractive personality: 'I rather avoid [him] as a politician and pressman'. Thomas Jones, *Whitehall Diary 1916–1925* (London, 1969), p. 21.

85. *My Political Life*, II, pp. 92 and 94.

of Public Safety' consisting of only five men, Lloyd George, Milner, Lord Curzon, Bonar Law and Arthur Henderson. The last two were the Conservative and Labour Party leaders. Curzon had served as Viceroy of India 1899–1905 and as a member of the Asquith coalition 1915–16. Amery came into contact with him especially on the question of war aims in the Middle East and Africa. Curzon held clear ideas on these issues and the consistency of his point of view contrasted with the unpredictable outlook of the Prime Minister, whom Amery regarded as mercurial and erratic. Nevertheless Amery recognized Lloyd George as a political genius with 'driving power and enthusiasm'.[86] He possessed a public presence, sometimes demagogic, and a spontaneity that Milner lacked. Amery relished a sketch by his colleague in the Secretariat, Sir Mark Sykes, who once drew a picture of Lloyd George as a rogue elephant with Curzon and Milner as elephants of a different species:

[T]runk in air, trumpeting . . . [Lloyd George] charged through the jungle. Curzon, as a Maharajah's state elephant, with a jewelled bracelet on his forefoot and a richly caparisoned howdah on his back, padded majestically behind. Milner just wearily leaned his great elephantine brow against a tree trunk, waiting for the rogue's state of 'must' to subside.[87]

Technically Amery was merely a Political Secretary (alongside Sir Mark Sykes). But he saw the position as part of an elite group of experts who would provide the

86. *Diaries*, I, p. 118.
87. *My Political Life*, II, p. 99.

members of the War Cabinet with ideas.[88] Milner was, above all, an administrator with a set of principles and a transcendent intellect. He welcomed Amery's effervescent suggestions and they grew ever closer. With Curzon, however, Amery maintained only a fragile intellectual rapport. Curzon had his own ideas.

At Milner's instigation, Amery prepared the groundwork for the Imperial Conference of 1917. The underlying idea, he wrote to William Morris Hughes, the Prime Minister of Australia, was to enlarge the 'Committee of Public Safety' by calling upon the half dozen or so 'strongest men in the Empire' to ensure victory and to plan for the peace.[89] Those who attended the conference in March included Borden of Canada, Massey of New Zealand, and Smuts of South Africa. Amery thus found himself, he reflected later, 'at the very heart of great events and in daily touch with great men'.[90] The Imperial Conference settled in Amery's own mind once and for all the debate with Lionel Curtis over federation. The year 1917 was the watershed.[91] The British Empire was now on the path towards equal and sovereign Dominions. Yet Amery was convinced that the emerging pattern of cooperation between the Dominions could be just as effective as that of

88. He was also responsible during the latter part of the war for much of the systematic preparation of the historical, economic, and geographical 'background handbooks' that were used by the British delegation at the Paris Peace Conference. See Erik Goldstein, *Winning the Peace: British Diplomatic Strategy, Peace Planning, and the Paris Peace Conference 1916–1920* (Oxford, 1991), pp. 22, 49, and 279.

89. Amery to Hughes, 8 January 1917, Amery Papers.

90. *My Political Life*, II, p. 175.

91. Hughes wrote to Amery: 'the Conference . . . was in itself a cornerstone, if not *the* cornerstone, in the Imperial temple.' Hughes to Amery, 9 July 1917, Amery Papers.

a formally unified system.[92] He was partly persuaded because of the warmth of sentiment that developed between two antagonists of the Boer War, Milner and Smuts. 'Great fun', Amery wrote, 'to see Lord M. and Smuts hobnobbing like the best of old friends.'[93] There was a principle underlying the conviviality. In the tradition of George Canning a century earlier, Amery was evoking the new world on the frontiers of the Empire to redress the balance of the old. 'Every nation for itself and God for us all' might well have been Amery's motto for the new Commonwealth system.[94] In any case he was exuberantly optimistic. The course of the war seemed to demonstrate a profound historical principle of free government. In Amery's words, 'Lord Durham had built better than Bismarck.'[95]

Amery was not a Germanophobe. He wished to break the back of 'aggressive Prussianism' but opposed a vindictive anti-German settlement. By virtue of geographical position and economic strength, Germany would always be a leading power in Europe. What concerned him was stability. He looked at Europe through the eyes of a British Imperialist. What political configuration might best serve British interests? He favoured a compromise peace that would leave most of south and central Europe in the Austro-German orbit—thus preserving in a 'solid rump'

92. Amery's ideas did not go down well with some of the Round Tablers. 'Amery got talking a lot of rot & quite spoilt the meeting', an Australian recruit, Frederic Eggleston, wrote in 1917. Warren G. Osmond, *Frederic Eggleston: An Intellectual in Australian Politics* (London, 1985), p. 85.

93. '[I]t was nice to see Smuts taking Lord M.'s arm and walking along with him, with the sort of affectionate deference that one would pay to a favourite uncle. Oom Alfred!' *Diaries*, I, pp. 145 and 161.

94. This is Hancock's speculation. See *Smuts*, I, p. 459.

95. *My Political Life*, II, p. 15.

the 'three main elements, German, Magyar and Slav'.[96] He thought it natural that Germany would be the dominant power in eastern Europe, and he foresaw the emergence of a European trading bloc led by Germany. German economic predominance in Europe might complement Britain's in the Empire and what eventually became known as the sterling area. Amery would not have opposed, as he later expressed it, 'the creation of some sort of loose Central European union in which Germany could find an economic sphere, a *Lebensraum*, and scope for political co-operation.'[97] With these views he remained fairly constant for some two decades until the annexation of Austria and the Munich crisis. This has a bearing, as will be seen, on Amery's position in the 'Milner group' at All Souls. At the end of the First World War Milner's disciples—and above all Milner himself—favoured a peace of reconciliation. This disposition of intellect and political proclivity helps to link the wartime period with the later era of appeasement. Amery's own ideas crystallized in 1917, the year of the Russian Revolution and the entry by the United States into the war. He believed that President Wilson's slogan of 'self-determination' was a shallow answer to the problems posed by Bolshevism in Russia and nationalism in eastern Europe. The British did not go to war to uphold the rights of Czechs, Poles, or Rumanians. The British, in Amery's view, were fighting the war to preserve the security of the British Empire.

'The object of British policy', he wrote in April 1917, 'can still be defined, as Pitt defined it in the great revolutionary war, by one word "security".' By security Amery

96. Ibid., III, p. 259.
97. Ibid., II, p. 162.

meant the guarantee for peaceful development of the British Dominions and colonies, which were the source of British power. In explaining the development of the British Empire he also explained the dynamic of British political influence: 'It is this continuous creation of new sources of power in new worlds overseas to redress the balance of the Old World which is the really characteristic feature of British policy, and accounts for the fact that an essentially defensive policy has led to the acquisition of immense Empire.'[98] To make the Empire secure, there was one indispensable condition. It recurred insistently in his memoranda and minutes. Germany must be stripped of her colonies. There was a corollary. Provinces of the Ottoman Empire must come under British control if they would help to secure a land corridor from Egypt to India.

Amery's official writings at this time establish a fair claim for him as the architect of the British geo-political system that endured until the crack-up at Suez in 1956. The basic idea was to establish an arc of British influence stretching from the Cape through East Africa and the Sudan to Egypt, from Egypt through the Middle East to India, and from India through South-East Asia to the Dominions in the antipodes. The return of any of the German colonies would threaten the new British system because of technological developments in submarine warfare. Here is the essence of Amery's case:

> The . . . German policy, that of sea power and colonial expansion at the expense of the British Empire, is, for the moment, defeated. But if Germany can recover her col-

98. Quoted in W.R. Louis, *Germany's Lost Colonies* (Oxford, 1967), p. 3. 'What we need', Amery wrote in the same vein, 'is our Monroe Doctrine for the whole of the region round the Indian Ocean from Cape Town to Wellington.' Amery to Hughes, 16 August 1918, Amery Papers.

onies, or even add to them as she hopes, by the annexation of Portuguese colonies, or by the control of the Congo, she will be able to renew it with far greater hopes of success. She will take effective military measures to make her colonies secure against conquest, and she will establish in each of them bases for submarines and raiders.

A base in Duala in the Cameroons, commanding the routes to South America and South Africa; a base in East Africa, whose radius covered the entrance to the Red Sea and threatened all communications between India and South Africa; one or more bases in the Pacific—once they are well organized the next war with the British Empire could be undertaken under far more favourable conditions.[99]

Amery had permanently in mind Mackinder's lesson of the heartland. He feared that Tanganyika, if left in German hands, might be linked with a 'Teutonised Turkey'. If Germany were to dominate the Middle East, this would threaten, in Amery's own words, 'our whole position in Egypt, India and the Eastern Seas.' Still worse, the Germans would then be certain to build a railway from Hamburg to Lake Nyasa—'the greatest of all dangers which can confront the British Empire in the future.'[100] In blocking this phantasmagoric German design, his geo-political ideas anticipated the territorial settlement at the close of the war. To offset the danger of a European power dominating the Eurasian land mass, the British Empire would extend contiguously from Africa through Asia and would

99. Memorandum by Amery, 'Notes on Possible Terms of Peace', G.T.-448, Secret, 11 April 1917, CAB 24/10. '[T]he most dangerous amateur strategist we have got', was a War Office comment on Amery's geo-political ideas. Quoted in Keith Jeffery, *The British Army and the Crisis of Empire 1918–22* (Manchester, 1984), p. 133.

100. Quoted in Isaiah Friedman, *The Question of Palestine 1914–1918* (London, 1973), pp. 173–72.

be linked by naval and air bases. Amery helped to secure, in his own language, 'that Southern British World which runs from Cape Town through Cairo, Bagdad and Calcutta to Sydney and Wellington. . . .'[101]

Any comment on Amery and the close of the First World War must emphasize the Middle East because of his commitment to Zionism. The creation of the state of Israel in 1948 was a tangible outcome of decisions made during the war in which Amery participated. Zionism also has a tangential connection with the theme of All Souls as an intellectual élite regarded by some as tantamont to a secret society. The point deserves to be reiterated while bearing in mind the *Zeitgeist* of Amery's political assumptions. The early twentieth century was the heyday of secret societies. Amery overestimated the influence of the Jews in 1917 just as others certainly held exaggerated ideas about the influence of All Souls. He believed that the Jews in Russia, Germany, and the United States had secret links in the affairs of finance and government. Like others in the British government, he thought that the outcome of the war might be determined by Jewish influence helping, for example, to bring the United States into the war on the side of Britain. On this point Amery's ideas were by no means original. On the contrary, they were representative of the time.

Amery's originality consisted in seeing clearly and com-

101. Amery to Lloyd George, 8 June 1918, Lloyd George Papers F/2/1/24. Nor were Amery's ambitions limited to the Southern Hemisphere. He wrote later: 'Both Iceland and Greenland ought to come into the Empire some day and provide a north-about bridge with Canada. Iceland's present status vis-à-vis Denmark is that of a British Dominion, but one very disposed to break off, and I see no reason why the Icelanders might not be tempted to come in as a Small Dominion under our umbrella!' Amery to Sir Samuel Hoare, 14 March 1928, Amery Papers.

prehensively the way in which Zionism might serve British interests in the Middle East. By 1917 the British were caught in a web of contradictory promises about the future of the region. They were committed through the Sykes-Picot agreement to partition the former Ottoman territories into shades of British and French influence. The British had given assurances, in a nebulous way, on Arab independence.[102] Amery approved of the ambiguity of these arrangements. In March of that year he met the official principally responsible for the Arab side of the question, Sir Henry McMahon. 'He is not very impressive, [and] has a very small head,' Amery wrote, 'but evidently [has] a lot of sense in it.'[103] Step by step it would become apparent, in Amery's own words, that 'The Arabs trust us and dislike the French'.[104] He was not under any illusion of Arab friendship, but merely meant that the Arabs and British could work together in self-interest to create a series of Arab states that would serve, in his phrase, as 'buffers' against the French or any other potential enemy. Here again Amery's mind was anticipating the lines of the peace settlement in the Middle East with the mandated territories of Syria and Lebanon under French supervision and Iraq and Palestine under British administration. Palestine was the cornerstone of the new system, in Amery's

102. For a recent analysis of these problems, see David Fromkin, *A Peace to End All Peace: Creating the Modern Middle East 1914–1922* (New York, 1989). 'What we want', he quotes from Amery, ' . . . is a British Monroe Doctrine which should keep that portion of the world free from future interference of ambitious powers.' (p. 358)

103. 17 March 1917, Amery MS Diary.

104. *Diaries*, I, p. 206. Amery wrote to Lord Curzon: 'We should leave it to the Arabs and Jews to advocate their own solution, which is certain to be one that suits us. This also has the advantage of putting on one side the French claims.' Amery to Curzon, 22 October 1918, Amery Papers.

view, because of its commanding strategic position.[105] He was thus alarmed at the suggestion that, to prove that territorial greed did not inspire British aims, the United States might be given Palestine as a mandate. Amery wrote to Lloyd George:

> To dump the Americans with their vigorous but crude ways into the middle of a problem like that of Palestine so closely connected with adjoining territories will be bound to lead to friction. . . . The great thing to aim at is a compact, continuous, easily defended and easily developed British Empire with the fewest friction surfaces with other Powers. If I had to give up territories it would not be Palestine or German East Africa but things like British Guiana, British Honduras, the Gambia, the Gold Coast, or even Gibraltar.[106]

In the event Britain held on to all of those territories. Amery's grand geo-political scheme remained intact.

What of Amery's Zionism? He was quite candid in saying that it was 'strategical' in origin. In other words, by a study of the map and the conflicting aims, he believed that the backing of the Jews in Palestine would benefit the new British Empire in the Middle East. 'I was keen on . . . establishing in Palestine a prosperous community bound to Britain by ties of gratitude and interest.'[107] Only after he had made this basic political judgement did he espouse the cause of Zionism itself. '[I]t was not long before I

105. 'Strategically Palestine and Egypt go together', Amery remarked to Lloyd George, because Palestine was 'a necessary buffer' to the Suez Canal. Quoted in Jeffery, *The British Army and the Crisis of Empire*, p. 123.

106. Amery to Lloyd George, 16 August 1918, Lloyd George Papers F/2/1/29. '[P]*lease don't set me down as a mere land grabber*', he emphasized to the Prime Minister.

107. *My Political Life*, II, p. 115.

realized what Jewish energy in every field of thought and action might mean for the regeneration of the whole of that Middle Eastern region which was once the home of the world's most ancient civilizations, and which in the course of centuries had gone derelict beyond hope of recovery by its own unaided resources.'[108] In the drafting of the commitment to the Jews in Palestine, the Balfour Declaration, Amery had a hand. He never exaggerated his claim to authorship of the Declaration, which he attributed to Sir Mark Sykes and others. But at a critical time, at Milner's suggestion, he did redraft it himself. Amery's version was:

> His Majesty's Government view with favour the establishment in Palestine of a National Home for the Jewish race [sic], and will use their best endeavours to facilitate the achievement of this object, it being clearly understood that nothing shall be done which may prejudice the civil and religious rights of the existing non-Jewish communities in Palestine or the rights and political status enjoyed by Jews in any other country who are contented with their existing nationality.[109]

Amery thus has a good claim to be regarded as one of the fathers of the state of Israel.

Did he ever have any second thoughts? One of Amery's strengths was not to look back. Once a decision had been taken, he stuck with it. He would not have agreed with

108. Ibid.

109. Ibid., p. 117. For Amery and the Balfour Declaration, see Michael J. Cohen, *Churchill and the Jews* (London, 1985), pp. 52–53; and Turner, *Lloyd George's Secretariat*, p. 79: 'Milner and Amery . . . sought to use Zionism as a bridgehead for British interests in the Middle East.' See also especially Mayir Vereté, 'The Balfour Declaration and Its Makers', *Middle Eastern Studies*, 6 (1970).

Elizabeth Monroe's famous statement that the Balfour Declaration was one of the greatest mistakes in Britain's Imperial history.[110] In his memoirs, however, he did issue a warning to the Israelis about the spiritual, cultural, and military forces of Zionism: 'It is upon its influence as a cultural mission, far more than upon its effectiveness as a militarist colony, that the ultimate success of Zionism will depend.'[111] At the time of the Balfour Declaration, Amery assumed, as did most of his colleagues, that Arab and Zionist goals were not incompatible. Through the rest of his career he demonstrated a capacity for reconciling Zionist aims with the idealism of the British Empire much in the same way that he always assumed that the purpose of All Souls would benefit that of the nation at large.

110. Elizabeth Monroe, *Britain's Moment in the Middle East* (London, 1963), p. 43.

111. *My Political Life*, II, p. 116.

II

The Royal Navy, the Empire, and Appeasement

1919–1939

I N THE 1920s AMERY briefly served as First Lord of the Admiralty and then for five years as Secretary of State for the Colonies and Dominions. He later played a part in the passing of the India Act of 1935 and took a stand in the controversy over appeasement. During the Second World War he was concerned not only with India but also with the question of Imperial Preference in connection with Anglo-American relations. In all of this period, and indeed throughout his career, he had an ambivalent attitude towards America. On the one hand, he warmly enjoyed welcoming Rhodes Scholars from the United States and encouraging them at a critical stage in their education. He served as a Rhodes Trustee from 1919 to 1955, thirty-six years. He missed only one meeting of the Rhodes Trust.[1] On the other hand, he mistrusted American economic and political power. Milner had written privately before the First World War about 'our own family', the British Empire: 'No doubt a great many Americans are thoroughly friendly to us, but a great number also are hostile. The best thing we can hope for is to keep on good terms with them. I neither anticipate, nor desire, anything more.'[2] Amery's attitude was identical.

Amery held two bedrock views about British security that were at variance with official policy. He did not believe in naval disarmament, or in the League of Nations.[3] At the Admiralty and at the Colonial Office he was obliged to preside over a course that he thought weakened the Empire. He held a Hobbesian view of international politics. He believed that the Germans and the Americans would respect only a strong Navy and a strong Empire. In his judgement, nothing would prevent Germany from eventually rearming. Thus it was realistic to try to keep on good terms. He was also wary of Japan. He saw the danger of driving Germany and Japan together as a common enemy. Thus he opposed any sort of alliance with the Soviet Union that might force Japan into Germany's arms. His view towards the United States was shaped not merely by the danger of American economic expansionism but also by the fickleness, in his opinion, of that amorphous phenomenon known as the American national

1. Papers of the Rhodes Trust, File 2698.
2. Milner to Colonel G.T. Denison, 3 November 1909, Milner Papers 36.
3. See Dick Richardson, *The Evolution of British Disarmament Policy in the 1920s* (London, 1989), e.g. pp. 24, 101, 199.

character. He agreed with Milner that it had a dangerous anti-British element in it. The termination of the Anglo-Japanese Alliance would put at risk the British Empire in the Far East. It was an illusion to believe that a comparable alliance, formal or informal, could be forged with the United States, and fatuous to think that a League of Nations could maintain the peace.

Immediately on assuming his responsibilities in the War Cabinet Secretariat during the war, Amery had come into conflict on those two points with Robert Cecil, then an Under-Secretary at the Foreign Office. Cecil stood for both the League of Nations and disarmament. It is useful to study one of Amery's letters to Cecil because it reveals the stark contrast in approach. Amery took an unabashed Imperialist stand. The British could not afford, he wrote, to be sentimental about 'giving back niggers to German rule.' He reiterated the tangible advantages to be gained from his basic geo-political idea of 'the elimination of Germany from the African, Indian Ocean and the Pacific Zones, and the creation of a belt of continuous British and British-held territory from Cape Town to Rangoon, encircling the Indian Ocean.' 'Guarantees' and 'reparations' would be impossible to achieve.[4] They were illusions of 'the Radical mind' or, even worse, sentiments reminiscent of 'the Squiff'. 'Guarantees for German good behaviour,' he wrote, 'leagues of peace, disarmament, etc.

4. Amery's views on reparations were brutally straightforward: 'the most important question . . . is to make sure that whatever the amount Germany does pay, we should get our fair share.' Quoted in Robert Skidelsky, *John Maynard Keynes: Hopes Betrayed 1883–1920* (London, 1983), p. 357. Here it is of interest to note that Amery gradually formed an adverse opinion of Keynes's theories. He later wrote of the *General Theory* that it was 'enveloped in a vast cobweb of abstract definition, eked out by algebraical formulas . . . [and] contains [only] a few commonplaces. . . .' *My Political Life*, I, p. 252.

are all fudge.' Cecil responded curtly. Amery's ideas, he wrote, represented everything that Britain was attempting to defeat—'pure Germanism'.[5]

Before Milner had moved to the Colonial Office as Secretary of State in 1919, he told Lloyd George that he would not accept the position unless Amery came with him. According to Amery's diary: 'He [Milner] said the only reason why he was taking the [Colonial] Office at all was to get me started in a position by the time he left public life to be able to carry on his ideas on Imperial matters.'[6] Amery thus became Parliamentary Under-Secretary at the Colonial Office as a result of Milner's influence, but it would be a mistake to assume that he owed everything to his mentor. Though he was identified as a Milnerite, Amery was in every sense his own man, intellectually independent and temperamentally resilient. His experience in the War Cabinet Secretariat had proved him to be extremely efficient. He could bring committees to conclusions and could effectively implement decisions.

As Under-Secretary at the Colonial Office (and as a prelude to his long stint as Colonial Secretary), Amery found himself involved in the work of the Paris Peace Conference in 1919. He was not favourably impressed with the knowledge of some of the statesmen. Lloyd George, he noted wryly in his diary, 'was much interested in dis-

5. *Diaries*, I, pp. 133–34. Amery once responded:
  'My dear Bob,
    You are always accusing me of aggressive Prussianism because of my reluctance to abandon places which seem to me essential for our security and where we have a better right than anyone else. But . . . I am sure we ought to try to settle the Middle-European situation in a constructive and not merely an anti-German spirit.'
                    Yours ever,
                    L.S.A. 21st Oct. 1918. [Amery Papers]
6. *Diaries*, I, p. 252.

covering New Zealand lay eastwards of Australia, he had always thought it was the other side!'[7] Amery recorded that observation in good humour. When he noted down his thoughts on President Wilson, he became more exasperated: 'he is . . . stupider than I had imagined.'[8] The President did give the impression of being 'less intractable and unreasonable' than Amery had previously believed, but that was as much as he would concede. The basic problem was 'the specious sham of world authority' that extended even to the colonies. Wilson insisted that the conquered colonies of Germany and the former territories of the Ottoman Empire be placed under the mandates system of the League of Nations. Rationally, Amery could prove to his own satisfaction that the influence of the League would amount virtually to nothing. 'I have a sneaking feeling myself', he wrote, 'that it really makes no difference as long as we actually get our flag up and our administration in. . . .'[9] On the other hand, the very mention of the phrase 'Mandates of the League', or later 'Trusteeship Territories' of the United Nations, aroused in Amery, as it did in Churchill, an almost irrational response. On this issue Amery and Churchill saw eye to eye: neither the League, the United Nations, nor the United States had any business meddling in the affairs of the British Empire. After the First World War Amery protested against the creation of the mandates system and during the Second World War he was still trying to abolish it—'that relic of the previous war', he would exclaim![10]

In Paris in 1919 he worked mainly on the peace settle-

7. Ibid., p. 240.
8. Ibid., p. 253.
9. Ibid.
10. See W.R. Louis, *Imperialism at Bay* (Oxford, 1977), p. 224 *et passim*.

ment in Africa. Here he found a man of kindred spirit in
George Louis Beer, Wilson's colonial expert. Beer was a
rara avis, an American Milnerite.[11] A historian from Co-
lumbia University, he had written books on the British
Empire in the eighteenth century and had come to admire
the evolving system of British colonial administration. It
is revealing about the extent of Milner's influence that he
managed to arrange for Beer to be the first permanent
secretary of the mandates section of the League of Nations, but Beer died in 1920.[12] At the Peace Conference
Beer and Amery united in common cause against the Belgians. Amery believed, like Beer, that it was absurd for
the Belgians to walk away with a valuable part of East
Africa, Ruanda-Urundi, simply because they had overrun
the region when the Germans had departed. Milner in-
dulged the Belgians far more than Amery or Beer thought
desirable by agreeing to the Belgian administration of
Ruanda-Urundi as a League mandate. 'I must confess',
Amery wrote in his diary, 'the Chief [Milner] has been
extraordinarily generous to the Belgians.'[13] Towards the
French, Amery and Beer held slightly different attitudes.
The French wished to annex the conquered West African
territories and insisted on the right to raise troops in the
event of war. Amery explained the motive: 'The French
want nigger conscripts not against us but to hold down

11. Beer had been in touch with various members of the Round Table
group, including Lionel Curtis, Eustace Percy, and Reginald Coupland. See
W.R. Louis, 'The United States and the African Peace Settlement of 1919: The
Pilgrimage of George Louis Beer', *Journal of African History*, IV, 3 (1963).

12. 'There is no doubt', Milner wrote after Beer's premature death, 'that
Beer had a strong sense of the duty which the more advanced nations owe to
the more backward. . . . [H]e appreciated the spirit in which we were trying
to carry "the white man's burden." ' In *George Louis Beer: A Tribute to His
Life and Work in the Making of History and Moulding of Public Opinion* (New
York, 1924), pp. 128–29.

13. *Diary*, I, p. 262.

Arabs & Germans.'[14] As a realist, he recognized in French policy a clarity of purpose that he could only admire. On the other hand, Beer was genuinely appalled at French cynicism. To Amery the French aims merely represented self-interest.

The Milner-Amery partnership at the Colonial Office led eventually to a significant achievement in colonial development, though at the time their initiative ended in frustration. Milner and Amery favoured the extension of state enterprise. They wished to develop the Empire and to break decisively with the prevailing orthodoxy of *laissez-faire*. To the House of Commons Amery spoke of the need for capital investment and the duty of the trustee to help the natives. There was no contradiction in those aims. Milner and Amery believed in the 'natural harmony' between the colonies and the metropole and refused to acknowledge that any conflict could arise because of development. Using the same language as in the period of reconstruction in South Africa, Amery emphasized that 'we cannot develop them [the colonies] and help them without an over-spill of wealth and prosperity that would be an immense help to this country. . . .'[15] The problem was that there was no prospect at all of money from the Treasury. When it became clear that there was no hope

14. Minute by Amery, 2 February 1920, CO 649/21; quoted in W.R. Louis. 'The Beginning of the Mandates System, 1919–1922', *International Organization*, XXIII, 1 (1969). Amery's language as well as his attitude was virtually identical with Lloyd George's: 'Mr. Lloyd George said that as long as M. Clemenceau did not train big nigger armies for the purpose of aggression . . . he was free to use troops.' *Foreign Relations of the United States: Paris Peace Conference 1919*, IX, p. 543.

15. Quoted in Stephen Constantine, *The Making of British Colonial Development Policy, 1914–1940* (London, 1984), p. 45. This is a key work, but for Amery and the question of development, see also especially J.M. Lee and Martin Petter, *The Colonial Office, War, and Development Policy* (London, 1982); and Kenneth Robinson, *The Dilemmas of Trusteeship* (London, 1965).

for 'a forward policy of Colonial development', Milner resigned in February 1921. But the initial impulse towards the Colonial Development Act of 1929 can be found in the Milner-Amery period at the Colonial Office.

Amery overlapped with the new Colonial Secretary, Churchill, for six weeks in 1921. During this time Amery brought to a conclusion, as far he could, projects that he had launched on strengthening the Colonial Service, assisting emigration to the Dominions, promoting Maltese self-government, and finishing the campaign against the 'Mad Mullah' in Somaliland. He delivered the final blow against the Somalis with a squadron of a dozen airplanes from Egypt.[16] Churchill now elevated Amery's military strategy almost to a doctrine: the British Middle East would be ruled with airplanes and armoured cars, thereby cutting costs and imposing a Victorian administrative parsimony at the Colonial Office. He independently shared Amery's views on Zionism. Churchill stated to an Arab delegation in March 1921 that a 'national home' for the Jews in Palestine 'will be good for the world, good for the Jews, good for the British Empire, but also good for the Arabs who dwell in Palestine. . . .'[17] Both Churchill and Amery were representative of their time in believing that a natural harmony of interests would prevail.

On one point they differed over an evaluation of personality. Churchill trusted T.E. Lawrence—Lawrence of Arabia—and appointed him as his adviser on Arab affairs. Lawrence's part in the Arab uprising against the Turks had fired his imagination. Amery was consistently more

16. Amery commented later on Iraq: 'If the writ of King Faisal runs effectively throughout his kingdom it is entirely due to British aeroplanes. If the aeroplanes were removed tomorrow the whole structure would inevitably fall to pieces.' Peter Sluglett, *Britain in Iraq 1914–1932* (London, 1976), p. 91.

17. Fromkin, *A Peace to End All Peace*, p. 519.

sceptical of Lawrence, though he acknowledged his charm. There is an entry in Amery's diary dated 2 May 1920, when Lawrence was a Fellow of All Souls:

> (All Souls College, Oxford): [T.E.] Lawrence was in the smoking room too last night and very entertaining in his quiet shy way. He gets called at 11 a.m., never breakfasts or lunches and very rarely appears at dinner—a quaint elusive creature altogether.[18]

As the diary progresses, Amery's notes become increasingly disenchanted. 'A very strange creature', Amery wrote three years later, 'mad'. Amery noted still later that Lawrence had explained that 'he was some very exalted person's natural son.'[19] Amery was not judgemental, but neither was he, as was Churchill, pro-Lawrence. Amery reiterated his impression of Lawrence much later by stating that he was 'a curious person'.[20] '[H]e was a strange, elusive creature, unsure of himself, alternating between extreme shyness and dislike of publicity, and a no less keen desire that his achievement should be known.'[21] Of greater importance, Amery's diaries reveal no trace of enthusiasm for Lawrence's idea that the Arabs should become 'a brown Dominion'. Lawrence envisaged a system of alliances between the Arab countries whereby they

18. *Diary*, I, p. 267. Amery had not taken the initiative in Lawrence's election as a Fellow. This was the work of Geoffrey Dawson. See John E. Mack, *A Prince of Our Disorder* (London, 1976), p. 277, more recently confirmed by Jeremy Wilson, *Lawrence of Arabia* (New York, 1990), p. 616.

19. *Diary*, I, pp. 319 and 330.

20. Amery to Basil Liddell Hart, 25 January 1954, Liddell Hart Papers 1/14.

21. *My Political Life*, II, p. 249. Amery took care to give a fair, final judgement, writing that Lawrence was 'essentially sane and well balanced' on Arab affairs and that he had 'a touch of genius that might have found an even greater opportunity in the Second World War than in the First.' Ibid.

would become part of the British Empire for military security and protection, but would remain autonomous within it. Amery, by contrast, was pro-Zionist and saw Palestine as a cornerstone of the British Empire; but he underestimated the potential damage to relations with the Arabs.

After Churchill became Colonial Secretary, Amery moved in 1921 to the Admiralty as Parliamentary and Financial Secretary, an important promotion. Here was another brief apprenticeship, this one as prelude to his service as First Lord of the Admiralty. Part of his new duties included preparation for the Imperial Conference of 1921, when the Prime Ministers of the Dominions met with members of the British Cabinet to decide whether or not to renew the Anglo-Japanese Alliance. This was a turning point in Imperial and naval affairs. If the alliance were continued, Britain would face the danger of an armaments race with the United States as a potential enemy. If it were terminated, the new basis of Britain's strategic and world policy would rest on the principle of arms limitation and an implicit understanding with the United States. As a junior minister, Amery did not take part in the debate in the Cabinet. But it is important to establish the nature of the controversy and to know where he stood. The issues went to the heart of his most passionate concern: the place of the British Empire in the world and how to protect Britain's military and commercial lines of communication. He came out, in his view, on the losing side of the argument. The alliance was not renewed. What were the consequences? Counter-factual theories of history sometimes give useful insight into underlying motives. In Amery's retrospective view, if the alliance with Japan had been renewed, the Empire in the Far East might have remained intact and Britain would have been in a far stronger position during the Second World War. Amery's instinct inclined him away from the United States and towards regional combinations that would ensure the security of the Empire. Later he held that it would not have been impossible for Britain to have cooperated with a European bloc under German leadership or an Asian bloc led by the Japanese—indeed, the British might have exerted a restraining influence.

As events transpired in 1921–22, he had to defend before Parliament the outcome of the Washington Conference on naval disarmament, which included the scrapping of twelve capital ships and a general reduction of the fleet. The British would now adhere to a one-power standard. In other words, they would maintain a fleet at least equal to any other fleet. But it was imperative not to fall below that level. Amery himself did not attend the conference, but he gave a full account of the reductions in the House of Commons:

> We have reached the limit. Things have been scraped to the bone. . . . We cannot go further unless, indeed, we abandon the one-power standard altogether, and drop to the rank of the second or third naval power—and if we drop once we shall do so for all time.
>
> We have no right to do that. We owe the maintenance of that standard to our fellow subjects in the Empire, with whom we formally, by resolution of the Empire Conference [of 1921], agreed only last summer that the standard of equality with any other Power was our minimum. . . . We owe it in trust to future generations of our people here and across the seas.

This was one of Amery's famous speeches. In his per-oration he eloquently reconciled the abandonment of Brit-ain's traditional predominance at sea with American friendship. But Britain must always remain at sea at least equal with the United States:

> We live and move and have our being as a nation and as an empire by our power to keep open and free the highways of the sea. That power we can never surrender even to the best friend or the closest ally. We have agreed at Washington to accept terms of equality in naval power with the one nation with which, above all things, we wish to live on terms of friendship. . . .[22]

Though Amery remained privately sceptical, he now took a robust public stand on Anglo-American relations and praised 'the wise daring of President Harding'. The 'Sceptre of Neptune' would now be taken up jointly by 'the great American nation' as well as by Britain, and the British should feel proud that 'the people of the United States' would ease the burden of policing the world. The spirit of Amery's comment was representative of his buoy-ant outlook in naval affairs. In assessing Amery's tenure of office at the Admiralty, Captain Stephen Roskill, the naval historian, has written: 'his unflagging energy, the enthusiasm with which he flung himself into the fray on behalf of the Navy, and above all his unashamed patri-otism, won him many friends in the service.'[23]

Amery became First Lord of the Admiralty in October 1922. He quickly established himself as one of the archi-tects of the Singapore strategy East of Suez. In the after-

22. *Parliamentary Debates* (Commons), 16 March 1922, cols. 2409–26.

23. Stephen Roskill, *Naval Policy Between the Wars: The Period of Anglo-American Antagonism 1919–1929* (London, 1968), p. 33.

math of the Washington Conference, it became clear to
Amery and others that it might be necessary to move the
reduced but modernized fleet rapidly from home waters
to the Indian Ocean or the Far East. This could not be
done without a major base in Asia. Singapore, situated
on the narrow strait between the Indian and Pacific
Oceans, was ideally placed. Might it provoke the Japanese? Amery answered that question by pointing out that
Singapore was no nearer Tokyo than Gibraltar was to
Boston. Could the British hold out if Singapore were attacked by the Japanese? Amery's answer here turned
again on distance:

> [G]iven the great distance of Singapore from Japan . . .
> given the presence of a swift it not very powerful squadron
> in Pacific waters, aided by long-range submarines, given
> the fact that the main fleet can go out normally in from
> four to six weeks, there is no reason to suppose that Sin-
> gapore could not hold its own against a powerful naval
> raid, or the raid of a navy with a small landing force such
> is likely to be directed against it.[24]

Against a Japanese assault by land, Amery confessed long
after the event in 1942, there was 'no sufficient answer'.[25]
Within the context of the time, however, the decision to
build the Singapore base seemed strategically sound. A
floating dock for capital ships, graving docks, wharves,
workshops, fuel storage tanks, ammunition dumps, bar-
racks, spacious mess quarters for officers, recreation fa-
cilities and hospitals—the plans for this gigantic arsenal
eventually helped to make the Singapore naval base the

24. Quoted in Correlli Barnett, *The Collapse of British Power* (London,
1972), p. 279.
25. *My Political Life*, II, p. 253.

major British dockyard east of Malta and one of the most magnificent naval installations in the world. Amery served as First Lord less than a year and a half. He unquestionably regarded the decision to build the Singapore base as his greatest naval accomplishment, though its implementation suffered grave delays. He wrote in January 1924: 'So ends my brief span of office as First Lord. . . . The shift of the main base of our Fleets away from the North Sea is now practically certain and I doubt whether even Singapore can be reversed.'[26] The plan for the redistribution of the fleet reinforced one of his basic geo-political ideas: 'In the Mediterranean, the true "middle sea", our battle fleet would be at the centre of the main highway of the Empire which ran from Halifax through the Straits of Gibraltar, the Suez Canal, and the Malacca Straits to Fremantle.'[27]

* * *

By the time of the 1923 election Amery had emerged in the public eye as the heir to Joseph Chamberlain. He had persuaded Stanley Baldwin and his colleagues that Imperial Preference would solve Britain's economic problems. They fought the campaign on this issue. It led to disaster, with a loss of eighty-eight Tory seats. The British people rejected tariff reform. Amery blamed Baldwin's campaign tactics of calling a snap election to fend off Lloyd George, but in any case it was a catastrophic setback for the cause of Imperial Preference. Amery's own career nevertheless prospered. He became Secretary for State

26. Amery MS Diary, 23 January 1924.

27. *My Political Life*, II, p. 273. For these ideas in broader context, see especially W. David McIntyre, *The Rise and Fall of the Singapore Naval Base* (London, 1979); and James Neidpath, *The Singapore Naval Base and the Defence of Britain's Eastern Empire 1919–1941* (Oxford, 1981).

for the Colonies in the Baldwin government of 1924–29. In 1925 he also assumed the office of Dominions Secretary. He made it a condition for his acceptance of service that he should be allowed to create a separate Dominions Office.[28] Amery's principal concern was to place the Dominions on the basis of equality with Britain. He played a vital part in the developments that led to the Statute of Westminster, the constitutional landmark in Dominion autonomy. His work in the Colonial Office can be illuminated by examining briefly two problematical territories, Palestine and Kenya, and further by his work with the Dominions that reached a critical point in the Imperial Conference of 1926. It is useful to bear in mind that during the time that Amery was Colonial Secretary, Churchill was Chancellor of the Exchequer.[29] On the question of finance they were at loggerheads throughout the period. 'Congenitally Little England', Amery remarked about Churchill after a year in office.[30]

The example of Palestine is of general interest because

28. See R.F. Holland, *Britain and the Commonwealth Alliance 1918–1939* (London, 1981), p. 44. Holland provides an illuminating quotation that helps to establish one of the motives. Amery wished to offset 'the legend of Colonial Office officials writing to a nigger one minute and then turning round and writing in the same strain to Dominion Prime Ministers'. (p. 32) It should also be noted that Amery did not have a high regard for the permanent officials of the Colonial Office. He wrote of G. V. Fiddes, the Permanent Under-Secretary: 'Fiddes . . . is a fatal influence, pretty narrow, appallingly irritating to any Dominion Statesman who gets near him or reads his telegrams. I imagine it must have been some ancestor of his who finally decided Benjamin Franklin that America's best hope lay in revolution.' Amery to Lloyd George, 14 November 1918, Amery Papers.

29. For some of the problems, see e.g. D.E. Moggridge, *British Monetary Policy 1924–1931* (Cambridge, 1972), pp. 207–08.

30. *Diaries*, I, p. 423. Amery moreover believed that Churchill failed to appreciate sufficiently the adverse balance of payments with the United States and the reasons why it was desirable to develop sources of supply including tobacco, cotton, tin, and rubber from the colonies. See Phillip Darby, *Three Faces of Imperialism: British and American Approaches to Asia and Africa 1870–1970* (New Haven, 1987), p. 129.

it reveals the type of society the British were attempting to mould out of the 'plural societies' in the Empire. The precedents of Canada and South Africa were imprinted on Amery's mind when he surveyed the problems of Arab and Jew in his trip to the Middle East within a few months of taking office. He was favourably impressed, as any visitor would have been, with the orchards and vineyards of the Jewish communities. 'I was much struck', Amery wrote, 'by the robust physique and virile appearance of these Jewish farmer settlers and by the health and good looks of the children.'[31] He recognized the value of Jewish collaboration. Only with Jewish assistance, and Jewish capital, could the harbour at Haifa be transformed into an industrial port, could a major airfield be built at Lydda, and a railway, he hoped, be constructed to Baghdad. Palestine as an Imperial asset was never absent from Amery's mind. 'The key position of this whole region is Palestine, which covers the Suez Canal from the North, and from which start the air route and future railway route from the Mediterranean to India.'[32]

Though Amery was a Zionist in the sense that he supported the idea of a Jewish national home in Palestine, he did not, in the 1920s, favour the creation of a Jewish state. He did, however, hope that the Jews of Palestine might develop an allegiance to Britain and the Commonwealth even though, of the 80,000 Jews in Palestine at the time, less than 0.5 per cent were English Jews. The majority came from Russia, Germany, Poland, and other eastern European countries. Even Amery sometimes found it hard to imagine these eastern European Zionists raising their glasses in a toast to an English King and a

31. *My Political Life*, II, p. 321.
32. Amery, *The Forward View*, p. 263.

British Commonwealth, but he remained cautiously optimistic.[33]

What type of society would emerge in Palestine? It had fallen to Churchill as Amery's predecessor as Colonial Secretary to elaborate the Balfour Declaration. Churchill had done so in 1922 by following the phraseology of the Balfour Declaration itself. The country of Palestine would not be a 'National Home' for the Jews but there would be a Jewish 'National Home' *in* Palestine. He then added a corollary. The rate of Jewish immigration would be determined by 'economic absorptive capacity'. Amery upheld those two principles of the national home and economic absorptive capacity, and he expounded them into a coherent explanation that also justified Britain's presence. The British administration would build the infrastructure of a state in which Arab and Jew would live harmoniously together, as others had—so it seemed at the time—in Canada and South Africa. Throughout his tenure as Colonial Secretary he tried to maintain a balanced attitude, making it clear that he was 'sympathetic to the Arabs and understood their point of view.' As for the Jews, they had to recognize that 'they must live with the Arabs who would probably always be the majority.'[34] He believed that the British could help to promote a common nationality—in his own words, that British policy should attempt to create 'a common Palestinian patriotism'. This was the idea of the bi-national state embodied eventually

33. See N.A. Rose, *The Gentile Zionists* (London, 1973), p. 79, where Amery is quoted as saying, guardedly, that he hoped Palestine might join the British Empire 'as a Dominion'. On another occasion he stated more frankly that 'we meant [for] Palestine in some way or other to remain within the framework of the British Empire.' Beloff, *Imperial Sunset*, II, p. 67.

34. *Diaries*, II, pp. 407–08. The best study of British policy during Amery's tenure as Colonial Secretary is Bernard Wasserstein, *The British in Palestine* (London, 1978).

in the White Paper of 1939 and the report of the Anglo-American Committee of Inquiry of 1946. Earlier in the 1930s he had adjusted his views to embrace the opposite solution of a separate Jewish state. He did not anticipate the unprecedented wave of Jewish immigration after 1933, but even by the end of his time in office in 1929 he was sceptical whether the majority of Arabs or Jews would accept a bi-national state. By the mid-1930s, in part because of conversations at All Souls with Reginald Coupland, Amery was willing to accept partition.[35] He now believed that a Jewish state would be a success.[36]

Amery was perturbed when the Chamberlain government in 1938 rejected the report of the Peel Commission recommending the division of the country between Arab and Jew, and he protested against the White Paper of 1939 which restricted Jewish immigration and aimed at preserving the approximate balance of the two-thirds Arab and one-third Jewish parts of the population. 'The Arabs will be with us [only] so long as they think we are strong enough to protect them against the Dictators', Amery wrote to Neville Chamberlain in 1939.[37] In Amery's view, the British government had again drifted into the contradictory promises of the First World war by guaranteeing Palestine to the Arabs while remaining committed to a Jewish national home.

Though Amery's subsequent involvement with Pales-

35. Coupland served on the Royal Commission of 1936–37 (the Peel Commission) and drafted the report favouring partition. Coupland was 'passionately sound on Colonies', Amery recorded in his diary, and 'very indignant' when the Chamberlain government refused to adopt the commission's recommendation of partition. (Amery MS Diary, 5 Nov. 1938) Amery wrote when the commission report was about to be published: 'Do give the Jews a fair chance.' (Amery to Coupland, 2 June 1937, Amery Papers)

36. See Rose, *Gentile Zionists*, p. 132.

37. Amery to Chamberlain, 16 May 1939, Amery Papers.

tine moves beyond the chronological scope of the interwar years, it is convenient to relate it here to demonstrate the consistency of his Zionist outlook. In 1943, when he was Secretary of State for India, Amery proposed to resolve the Palestine problem by allowing the Arabs to create their own independent state as a 'greater Syria' (encompassing Syria, Lebanon, Transjordan, Iraq, and Arab Palestine) and by giving the Jews an independent state (larger than the proposal put forward by the Peel Commission in 1937 but smaller than the actual state that emerged in 1948).[38] Amery pressed this solution at a Cabinet meeting on 2 July 1943.[39] 'Winston subsequently, to my delight, expressed his own conviction in the necessity of partition. . . .' This was a historic turning point. Amery wrote exuberantly that it was 'a great day for the Jews if they had known of it—perhaps some day they may include Winston with Balfour (and to some extent myself too) as one of their real friends.'[40]

Amery then helped to steer the partition scheme through the Palestine Committee of the Cabinet and to meet the objections of the Chiefs of Staff.[41] 'There is noth-

38. See especially Ronald W. Zweig, *Britain and Palestine During the Second World War* (London, 1986); and Gavriel Cohen, *Churchill and Palestine, 1939–1942* (Jerusalem, 1976); and by the same author, *The British Cabinet and Palestine April–July 1943* (Jerusalem, 1976; both of Cohen's books are in Hebrew but with documents in English). See also Bernard Wasserstein, *Britain and the Jews of Europe, 1939–1945* (London, 1979); and Michael J. Cohen, *Churchill and the Jews*.

39. W.M. (43) 92nd Conclusions, Minute 2, Confidential Annex, 2 July 1943, CAB 65/39.

40. *Diaries*, II, p. 897. Amery drew on some of the ideas put forward by a 'brilliant' Colonial Office official, Douglas Harris. See W.R. Louis, *The British Empire in the Middle East* (Oxford, 1984), pp. 41, 434, and 454–55.

41. The Foreign Office protested against Amery's inclusion on the Palestine Committee because of his pro-Zionist views, but Churchill successfully defended him: 'it is quite true that he has my way of thinking on this point . . . but he has great knowledge and mental energy.' Cohen, *Churchill and the Jews*, p. 254.

ing the Arabs can do', he wrote to Churchill, 'beyond flag-waving. . . .'[42] Amery wished to make the partition quick and decisive. 'The only thing that can make a judgement of Solomon possible', he emphasized, 'is the swift and clean cut. What we cannot afford to do is to saw away slowly at the squealing infant in the presence of two hysterical mothers and amid the ululations of a chorus of equally hysterical relations in the Arab and the Jewish world.'[43] Churchill agreed with Amery. They reinforced each other's views. One wonders how the momentum towards partition might have affected the postwar political configuration of the Middle East had the partition plan not been halted by the assassination of Lord Moyne by Zionist extremists in November 1944. Moyne was Minister Resident in the Middle East and one of Churchill's close friends. 'It is tragic', Amery wrote in his diary, 'that a man of such devotion to duty and kindliness to all men should be murdered by insane fanatics who have inflicted a possibly fatal injury on their own cause.'[44] Thus Amery was disheartened at the close of the Second World War when his efforts at nation building in the Middle East seemed to founder on elements of communalism that had frustrated, in a different way, his efforts in Africa.

* * *

The example of Kenya throws light on Amery's plans for the building of states within the British system in Africa. Like Cecil Rhodes earlier, Amery saw the natural development of small units into larger configurations, territories into federations. In eastern and central Africa, federation

42. Amery to Churchill, 'Most Secret', 24 January 1944, Amery Papers.
43. Amery to Churchill, 'Most Secret', 22 January 1944, Amery Papers.
44. *Diaries*, II, p. 1018.

might be linked with federation. He sympathized with the white settlers who believed that eastern Africa for the indefinite future would be ruled by the British. He once responded favourably to Philip Kerr's view 'that the Rhodesias and East Africa are destined to go through the same phases of white development as S. Africa and that it is therefore very desirable that they . . . should learn something from the mistakes made by their precursor.'[45] Kerr believed that black and white should develop together, with black Africans given representation north of the Zambezi. For the long-range future Amery upheld the idea of 'a wider Dominion of British African States'. Thinking of Kenya, he once paraphrased Carlyle that East Africa was 'the ground plan of the universe.'[46] Here was a magnificent opportunity for planned economic development of harbours, railways, roads and air routes, post office and telegraph services—the infrastructure of the modern state. This development could take place far more efficiently within a federated East Africa than with Kenya, Tanganyika, and Uganda each pursuing separate ways.

Amery did not have a free hand. He had inherited one of the most emphatic declarations of policy ever penned, the Kenya White Paper of 1923. The crucial passage read:

Primarily, Kenya is an African territory, and His Majesty's Government think it necessary definitely to record their considered opinion that the interests of the African natives must be paramount, and that if, and when, these

45. Amery MS Diary, 10 February 1927.
46. Amery, *The Forward View*, pp. 256 and 259.

interests and the interests of the immigrant races should conflict, the former should prevail.[47]

This was a policy actively supported by Sir Frederick (Lord) Lugard, who in 1922 had published *The Dual Mandate* upholding the principles of trusteeship as opposed to the rights claimed by the white settlers—for example, those in Kenya led by Lord Delamere. Amery found Lugard tediously persistent in stirring up public sentiment for safeguarding the rights of the Africans.[48] The question was how to pursue federation without violating the pledge of African paramountcy.

Amery attacked the problem as he had in the controversy with Lionel Curtis over Imperial Federation. First make economic progress, then political development would be possible. He pressed forward with the plan for closer economic union. In early 1925 he appointed Sir Edward Grigg as Governor of Kenya. Grigg, as has been mentioned, was a member of the Round Table group and one of Amery's close friends. Grigg now tried to assemble a new Kindergarten.[49] He held a vision of Kenya as a colony that would attract an ever-increasing number of British settlers, thus ending dependence on African labour. Amery tried to temper Grigg's plans such as the 'scheme for dividing up Kenya into [a white] self-

47. See Robert G. Gregory, *India and East Africa* (Oxford, 1971), chap. 7. For useful perspective on Amery in this and other episodes, Partha Sarathi Gupta, *Imperialism and the British Labour Movement 1914–1964* (London, 1975).

48. Lugard himself, Amery wrote, was 'very much opposed' to self-rule by the white settlers in Kenya 'but otherwise sound in his views.' Amery MS Diary, 2 December 1930.

49. Notably by the recruitment of R. Feetham, a South African judge who had been a member of Milner's Kindergarten. 'In the end . . . the kindergarten idea fell through.' George Bennett, *Kenya: A Political History* (London, 1963), pp. 58–59.

government area and [a] native reserve.'[50] Grigg's advocacy for closer union posed a political problem in England
as well as in East Africa. Amery secured Cabinet approval
in 1926 for the unification of the railways, harbours, and
steamships of Kenya and Uganda under Grigg's control,
but the Governor of Tanganyika, Sir Donald Cameron,
suspected that closer union might be the first step towards
domination of all of East Africa by white settlers. Amery
had to convince his colleagues in the Cabinet that closer
economic union was not only economically sound but
would not reverse the principle of 'native paramountcy'.
In May 1927 Amery walked around the Quad at All Souls
and discussed this problem with Lionel Curtis, in whom
Amery confided on questions of high policy. Curtis
thought that 'Ned [Grigg] was in too great a hurry and
the thing might be to send out a commission . . . to inquire
and frame a scheme on the spot.'[51] This was the birth of
the ill-fated Hilton Young Commission.

Appointed by Amery, this commission included Sir Edward Hilton Young, the chairman, who saw eye to eye
with Amery but was a man of such a philosophical and
detached temperament that he could not persuade the
other members to stick to the economic agenda. 'He is
not by any means sure he will carry his colleagues with
him', Amery warned Grigg.[52] The India Office had insisted
on the appointment of an Indian Civil Servant, Sir Reginald Mant. But Mant was not the source of trouble for
the federationists. Amery had appointed two members
whom he regarded as a safe bet, Sir George Schuster,
then serving as a financial adviser in the Colonial Office,

50. *Diaries*, I, p. 414.
51. Ibid., p. 506.
52. Amery to Grigg, 16 May 1928, Sir Edward Grigg Papers.

and J.H. Oldham, the Secretary of the International Missionary Council. It turned out to be a rogue commission. Instead of following Amery's lead on economic problems, they reopened the political question. Rather than concentrating exclusively on the plan for economic union, they reiterated the policy of African paramountcy. Oldham and Schuster believed that their report should emphasize not merely economic problems but those of political power. They raised basic questions of 'What is Kenya?' and 'Who are the people of Kenya?' Their report destroyed the vision of Kenya as white man's country by stating that the immigrant communities of British and Indians could at best aspire to 'partnership', not self-government on the model of Southern Rhodesia. Despite his attempt to salvage it, Amery's Kenya policy at the end of his tenure was a pronounced failure.[53] The tide of closer union had turned, never again to rise.

The example of Kenya reveals much about Amery's approach to the problem of creating viable nation-states in Africa. The questions 'What is Kenya?' and 'Who are the people of Kenya?' were precisely the ones that he regarded as unrealistic and dangerous. He did not wish to regard Kenya as a 'separate personality', he wrote to Grigg, but rather as an administrative or geographical division to be shaped as part of East Africa.[54] It is noteworthy that in African questions of the 1920s Amery took a robust Imperialist line similar to Churchill's, and indeed he endorsed Churchill's famous earlier statement that

53. Amery himself believed that he had managed to set his East African policy back on tracks towards federation. 'I only hope the new [Labour] Government won't wreck it', he wrote in June 1929. He noted later, 'They did.' *Diaries*, I, p. 598.

54. Amery to Grigg, 'Private & Pesonal', 15 April 1926, Sir Edward Grigg Papers.

Kenya would become 'a characteristically and distinctively British colony, looking forward in the full fruition of time to responsible self-government.' Amery himself continued to believe that the 'destiny' of Kenya 'rested with the white settler'.[55] Even Reginald Coupland, despite a meeting of minds with Amery on most subjects, feared that he would 'stampede the Cabinet and get a pro-Delamere policy adopted.'[56] Tropical Africa remained to Amery a backward region best ruled and developed by the white man, in comparison with other parts of the Empire where he had more progressive views. In the Middle East, particularly in Palestine, he was quicker to apply the signal lesson he had learned from the Boer War. The fate of different peoples cannot be dictated. Peoples of different 'races' cannot be manipulated. They must determine their future among themselves and by themselves.

Amery was in his element in dealing with the white Dominions. One of his finest moments—to be ranked along with his urging Neville Chamberlain to go in 1940 —was his handling of the Imperial Conference of 1926 when the representatives of the Dominions and the members of the British Cabinet resolved the problem of constitutional status. Amery in 1926 turned fifty-three and was at the height of his powers. He had worked towards the outcome of the conference even before he assumed his duties at the Colonial and Dominions Offices not only by exhaustive conversation but also by extensive correspondence with friends in Australia, New Zealand, Canada, and South Africa. 'While we do not want anything in the nature of a fixed or written constitution for the British Commonwealth', he wrote to Smuts in 1921, 'we

55. Gregory, *India and East Africa*, p. 329.
56. Jones, *Whitehall Diary*, II, p. 171.

do want a general agreement and public understanding on fundamentals. . . .'[57] When the conference opened in October 1926, all of Amery's theories were put to the test. Smuts was now out of office. The South African Prime Minister, General J.B.M. Hertzog, stated at the outset that the Dominions must have 'independent' status. The Canadian Prime Minister, W.L. Mackenzie King, retorted that 'independence' was an unacceptable word in Canada because it smacked of the American Revolution.[58] The constitutional fat was in the fire.

Amery was on excellent terms with Hertzog and even with Mackenzie King, though he had had acrimonious dealings with the latter on trade issues. The exchange of views by lengthy correspondence had helped to create an atmosphere of mutual trust.[59] The word 'independent' was dropped in favour of the famous phrase 'equal in status' suggested by Lord Balfour. Amery as usual played an important part in the drafting, this time by suggesting that another phrase, 'British Empire', was still useful because it covered colonies, protectorates, and mandated territories in a way that no other words could summarize. It would be a mistake to exaggerate Amery's contribution to what became known as the Balfour Report, but Han-

57. Jean van der Poel, ed., *Selections from the Smuts Papers* (7 vols., Cambridge, 1966–73), V, p. 78.

58. For King and Amery in the context of the 1926 conference, see Philip G. Wigley, *Canada and the Transition to Commonwealth* (Cambridge, 1977), chap. 8.

59. This at least was Amery's view, e.g.: 'I think I can take credit for having done a great deal with Hertzog since I first began to correspond with him on my appointment.' *Diaries*, I, p. 482. For Amery's part in the conference, see H. Duncan Hall, *Commonwealth: A History of the British Commonwealth of Nations* (London, 1971), *passim* but especially p. 611. Hall was the first historian to recognize the extent of Amery's influence. See also Ronald Hyam and Ged Martin, *Reappraisals in British Imperial History* (London, 1975), chap. 10, which is illuminating on Amery and Ireland and the conference of 1926 as well as Ireland generally, a theme I have not pursued here.

key, who was as fastidious with historical detail as he was with the contemporary record, later stated that he 'would not like to deny' Amery's part in developing the under- lying concept.[60] The Balfour Report on constitutional status—eventually embodied in 1931 in the Statute of Westminster—was so significant a milestone in Amery's career that the crucial passage should be quoted:

> Autonomous communities within the British Empire, equal in status, in no way subordinate one to another in any aspect of their domestic or external relations, though united by a common allegiance to the Crown, and freely associated as members of the British Commonwealth of Nations.

Amery himself quite accurately described Balfour's 'stroke of genius' in placing the definition within its his- torical and philosophical context, and in recognizing the strength of voluntary association. It was true, Amery re- flected after the final session, that the Balfour Report left open the way 'to dissolution'. 'That is a risk we have got to run and if the will to unity is there we shall overcome it.'[61] The Balfour formula became a tenet in his Imperial belief that liberty and equality could be reconciled with unity. In Sir Keith Hancock's words, the declaration jus- tified 'unlimited faith' in the Empire's future.[62] This was certainly true for Amery. The Balfour Report on consti-

---

60. Roskill, *Hankey*, II, p. 430, n. 5.

61. *Diaries*, I, p. 483. Donald Cameron Watt comments on this essential element of Amery's strategy: 'Leo Amery . . . worked hard to contain and divert the nascent nationalism of the white settler element in the Empire into a common support of British policy. . . .' D. Cameron Watt, *Succeeding John Bull: America in Britain's Place 1900–1975* (Cambridge, 1984), p. 48.

62. A 'teleological affirmation', in Hancock's memorable phrase. *Survey of British Commonwealth Affairs*, I, p. 285.

tutional status was, in Amery's own words at the close of the conference on his fifty-third birthday on 22 November 1926, 'one of the big things I have worked for most of my life.'[63]

* * *

After the fall of Baldwin's government in 1929, Amery did not hold office again until he joined Churchill's wartime coalition in 1940. He now used the House of Commons as his base of operations. In the 1930s he took an independent line, as might be expected, on Imperial Preference, but was initially frustrated by a pledge made by Baldwin not to introduce tariffs without a public mandate. Baldwin of course well remembered the catastrophe of 1923. Amery was excluded from the national government of 1931, in part because of Labour opposition, but there were other reasons. It is useful here to make a brief assessment of Amery at this stage of his career because it helps to understand why he never achieved his goal of becoming Prime Minister, why he played a less than major part in British politics of the 1930s, and why his influence in Imperial affairs was thus not as great as he had hoped.

He was exceedingly efficient in running his own departments, so much so that he freely offered advice to colleagues on their affairs. This advice was not always gratefully received. 'Why will Leo [Amery] insist', according to Cabinet gossip, 'on answering every speaker at Cabinet? Why does someone not pull his coat and stop him?'[64] He was becoming more and more garrulous, and, on the question of Imperial Preference, increasingly pugnacious. Austen Chamberlain, who served with him

63. *Diaries*, I, p. 482.
64. Jones, *Whitehall Diary*, II, p. 175.

throughout the Baldwin government in the 1920s, believed him to be 'a poor Parliamentarian, very unhandy so far in spite of his brains'.[65] In Cabinet discussion he was often ineffective, allowing his thoughts to ramble and often boring his colleagues.[66] The most damning comment was made by Baldwin himself in 1929: 'Amery does not add a gram to the influence of the government.'[67] Historians have made similar observations. Perhaps the most fair-minded is by Ronald Hyam of Cambridge:

Amery was one of the two or three best informed right-wing colonial secretaries Britain has ever had. To his admirers, he was a man of imaginative vision and fearless determination, alive to the demands of a new time, a dynamo of energy and a passionate believer in England's imperial mission. He never quite carried sufficient weight among his cabinet colleagues to secure easy implementation of his policies. Perhaps he talked too much: it is always fatal.[68]

Whatever might be said of his loquacity, no one could deny that his willingness to address Imperial issues made

65. Keith Middlemas and John Barnes, *Baldwin* (London, 1969), p. 126.

66. After 1929 Amery and Lord Beaverbrook worked together in loose alliance on Imperial Preference. There is an undated note written in Beaverbrook's handwriting in his papers on Amery's style as a publicist: 'dull, academic, without anything fresh'. (Beaverbrook Papers C/6) A.J.P. Taylor makes a similar point about Amery in the Cabinet: 'if the truth be told, he was, though able, a long-winded bore and those with whom he had sat in cabinet must have rejoiced that he did so no longer.' *English History 1914–1945*, p. 327.

67. Jones, *Whitehall Diary*, II, p. 180. The Earl of Birkenhead, who was then Secretary of State for India, summed up his impressions of Churchill and Amery by exclaiming that Churchill was 'Often right, but my God when he's wrong!!'—and by dismissing Amery merely with the phrase 'Always wrong.' John Campbell, *F.E. Smith: First Earl of Birkenhead* (London, 1983), p. 792.

68. Ronald Hyam, *The Failure of South African Expansion* (London, 1972), p. 102. On Amery's general lack of political influence, see also especially Philip Williamson's incisive *National Crisis and National Government* (Cambridge, 1992), pp. 49, 243 *et passim*.

him the foremost spokesman on the British Empire. In 1927–28 he became the first Colonial Secretary ever to visit all of the white Dominions, travelling over 55,000 miles and delivering some 300 speeches.[69] After the electoral defeat in 1929, he returned to Canada to scale Mount Amery, the peak of 10,940 feet named after him in the Canadian Rockies. Years later, during the Second World War, he was elected President of the Alpine Club. Here is a characteristic example of Amery's wit. He wrote in 1943: 'I have always regarded the Presidency of the AC and the Prime Ministership of the UK as the natural twin summits of [my] ambition'. '[I]t is something', he concluded, that he had achieved 'at any rate one of them.'[70]

It is also useful at this stage to establish Amery's view of Churchill mid-way through the interwar period and to study his later estimate of Churchill as a wartime leader —especially in contrast to Amery's assessment of his other great wartime leader, Lloyd George. In 1929 Churchill sailed with Amery on the same ship to Canada, the *Empress of Australia*. 'On essentials', Amery reflected after a long evening's conversation, Churchill ' . . . is still where he was 25 years ago.' 'He can only think in phrases and close argument is really lost on him.' The conversation had taken place in Churchill's cabin:

Towards the close of this discussion I got up to go and Winston to undress, ending in his putting on a long silk nightshirt and a woolly tummy band over it. W. asked why

69. See L.S. Amery, *The Empire in the New Era* (London, 1928). On his speeches, Lionel Curtis once wrote to Amery's wife, Bryddie: 'Leo made the most brilliant and witty after-dinner speech at All souls on Saturday night that I have ever heard. Why on earth does he not treat his public audiences now and then to this sort of thing if he can do it so well?' Curtis to Mrs. Amery, 5 November 1934, Amery Papers.

70. *Diaries*, II, p. 938.

I was smiling and I replied "Free Trade, Mid Victorian Statesmanship and the old-fashioned nightshirt, how appropriate a combination" and left him.

I have always said that the key to Winston is to realise that he is Mid-Victorian, steeped in the politics of his father's period, and unable ever to get the modern point of view. It is only his verbal exuberance and abounding vitality that conceal this elementary fact about him.[71]

That was a perceptive comment. Amery had insight into motivation and character and he was usually generous in his assessments of his contemporaries. Later he drew a comparison between Churchill and Lloyd George on the occasion of the latter's death in 1945:

The essence of the difference lies in the fact that Ll.G. was purely external and receptive, the result of intercourse with his ~ellow men, and non-existent in their absence, while Winston is literary and expressive of himself with hardly any contact with other minds.

Again Winston is a retrospective Whig of the period 1750–1850, with very little capacity for looking forward, while Ll.G. was a constructive Radical, with essentially the same kind of outlook, allowing for differences of upbringing, as Joe [Chamberlain] or Milner, or for that matter myself.[72]

Again, the judgement was astute, though Amery, writing in 1945, betrayed nostalgia for happier times, on the whole, with Lloyd George. By contrast Amery had battles royal with Churchill over Imperial Preference and India, two themes that run through the Amery-Churchill relationship from 1929 onwards.

71. Ibid., pp. 49–50.
72. Ibid., p. 1034.

Three years later Amery again found himself in Canada, this time for the Imperial Economic Conference at Ottawa. He was generally regarded as an out-of-office Tory with considerable influence in the House of Commons, though technically he represented the Central Chamber of Agriculture and the Empire Sugar Association. Churchill referred to the results of the Ottawa conference as 'Rottawa'.[73] Amery in part agreed with that judgement, but for the opposite reason. The economic accords reached at Ottawa by Britain and the Dominions in 1932 represented to Amery only a partial victory of what he called the 'national philosophy' of Imperial Preference over the countervailing school of Free Trade. From Amery's point of view the conference did not go far enough. He believed that the members of the Empire and Commonwealth should develop a common agricultural and industrial policy as well as a common currency. The circumstances of the Great Depression now presented the opportunity to forge an integrated Imperial economy. But the delegation representing the United Kingdom did not rise to the occasion. Amery participated only on the fringes of the conference. It was probably a mistake for him to attend at all. Well-meaning articles in the press represented him as the single intellect who truly understood the complexity of the economic issues. His presence was resented by the British delegates, especially Neville Chamberlain, the Chancellor of the Exchequer.

The British delegation believed that Amery was in collusion with the Dominion representatives. In fact he sat mainly in isolation in his hotel room, at a distance watching

73. For Amery and the conference, see Ian M. Drummond, *Imperial Economic Policy 1917–1939* (London, 1974); and, by the same author, *British Economic Policy and the Empire* (London, 1972).

the conference degenerate into haggling over wheat and meat. Amery bitterly recorded in his diary in August 1932:

> Neville . . . accused me of wrecking the Conference by inciting the Dominions to make impossible requests etc. If he knew how little 'inciting' I have done and how meekly I have hung about in the hope that I might be useful. . . . [T]hey are fastening on me as the devil in the whole business, the mysterious schemer who has been working things up to a deadlock. . . .
>
> The trouble is that they think I am on the side of the 'enemy', their whole mentality being subconsciously anti-Dominion.[74]

Amery believed at the time that a series of useful agreements would emerge from the conference, but that they would be negotiated in a spirit of mistrust and would leave 'an unpleasant taste in the mouth'.

In fact the Commonwealth governments at Ottawa achieved a great deal, but the results did not accord with the extravagant claims made by Amery and others for Imperial Preference. The tariff reformers argued that their policy would lead to Imperial strength and prosperity. But paradoxically the political results were more apparent than the economic consequences because of the suspicion stirred up in other countries, especially the United States. Sumner Welles, Roosevelt's Under Secretary of State during the early part of Second World War, later denounced the Ottawa accords as 'economic aggression'. Amery was outraged at this assessment. He could rightly point out that Britain and the Dominions had merely negotiated bilateral agreements on timber, metals, tobacco, wheat, beef, mutton, lamb, bacon, sugar, cocoa, coffee, fish, ap-

74. *Diaries*, II, p. 253.

ples. Amery's obsession with such commodities no doubt demonstrated to the Americans of the time that the British had a large appetite, but in his own view the Ottawa accords were by no means as effective or far-reaching as they might have been under inspired leadership in 1932. Still, he believed at the time that 'a great change in our national and Imperial policy had taken place.'[75] The British government had at last adopted a programme of tariff reform.

In the 1930s a substantial change also took place in Britain's relationship with India. Having been born in India, Amery had taken pride in the Raj since childhood. His interest in the subcontinent was peripheral as compared with the attention he paid to the white Dominions, but the theme of India can be found as a thread running consistently through his conversations, especially at All Souls. Lionel Curtis helped to shape Amery's ideas, notably during the period of the First World War when Curtis had proposed Indian self-government in the provinces. Curtis's 'grasp of the principle of government is in extraordinary contrast to the muddle-headedness of most of our statesmen', Amery had written in 1918.[76] At All Souls Amery later debated Indian issues with (Sir) Maurice Gwyer, who helped to draft the India Act of 1935 and became Chief Justice of India in 1937, and (Sir) Penderel Moon, the most distinguished of All Souls scholars on India. Amery first came into contact with the latter when Moon was a young Fellow before entering the Indian Civil Service. Amery also discussed Indian issues with Edward

75. *My Political Life*, III, pp. 94–95. For Amery's reasoned public views at the time, see especially L.S. Amery, 'The Imperial Economic Conference: Before the Meeting at Ottawa', *International Affairs*, XI, 5 (September 1932).

76. Amery MS Diary, 4 May 1918.

Wood, later Lord Halifax. Amery did not always hold him in high esteem. 'Edward Wood [is] a dignified exterior who says nothing', Amery once noted.[77] Nevertheless it was Halifax who, as Viceroy of India, forced Amery to crystallize his views about India's future. Halifax believed that the ultimate goal of British rule in India should be Dominion status. Amery now saw the logic of applying to India the same principles that he had worked out for the white Dominions—provided India would only gradually achieve equal status in the distant future. 'Personally I do not know that there is anything so terrible in that [principle] if the attainment of the goal is postponed long enough', he wrote. He added, as if slightly hoist on his own petard: 'it is difficult to see how responsible government can ever ultimately stop short of Dominion status.'[78] With that logical conclusion in mind, Amery worked wholeheartedly in favour of the India Act of 1935.

Bearing in mind the constitutional and political background of the 1935 Act, it is relevant to state briefly its purpose and to make clear the contrasting attitudes of Amery and Churchill.[79] The long-range design of the Act was to ensure the unity of India by establishing provincial self-government within a federal union. The more short-term purpose was to retain British supremacy over the Congress, the Muslims, and the Princes. The overriding intent was to keep India within the British Imperial system. The British would continue to control the vital areas of finance, security, and foreign affairs. Churchill, how-

77. Amery MS Diary, 9 November 1930.

78. *Diaries*, II, p. 52.

79. For Amery and the 1935 Act, see especially Carl Bridge, *Holding India to the Empire: The British Conservative Party and the 1935 Constitution* (London, 1986).

ever, resisted any form of Indian self-government heart and soul, with the rekindled passion of his nineteenth-century romanticism. According to Baldwin, 'Winston . . . wants . . . the Tory Party to go back to pre-war and govern with a strong hand. He has become once more the sub-altern of hussars of '96.' In Amery's own words, 'Winston is . . . a purely destructive element.'[80]

Amery argued that it was far wiser to meet the demand for self-government than to keep the safety valve screwed down. Sooner or later, India would come into the Com-monwealth as an equal partner. He worked closely with Sir Samuel Hoare, then Secretary of State for India, to secure the Bill's passage in the House of Commons. Amery and Hoare were close friends. Amery regarded him as intelligent, competent, and shrewd. Amery's diary paid tribute to 'Sam's constructive and essentially Con-servative mind.'[81] In defending Hoare against Churchill's onslaughts, Amery achieved his greatest oratorical victory over Churchill. Amery recalled it with glee the rest of his life and never allowed Churchill to forget it. Amery care-fully laid a trap with a Latin phrase, which he quoted in a debate on 13 June 1934, saying that Churchill himself had chosen it as a motto: 'Fiat justitia, ruat caelum'. Churchill rounded on him, demanding a translation. He wished to know the motto Amery attributed to him.

80. Amery to George Lloyd, 'Private & Confidential', 11 February 1931, Amery Papers. Lloyd had served as a Governor in India and as High Com-missioner in Egypt. On India he was a diehard. He once wrote to Amery: 'You see, if India goes, everything goes: our honour, our wealth, our strategic security and our prestige.' (Lloyd to Amery, 'Private', 10 Feb. 1931, Amery Papers) Amery responded that he would not attempt to answer by letter 'for that might put an end to all friendship.' (Amery to Lloyd, 'Private & Confidential', 11 Feb. 1931, Amery Papers). See John Charmley, *Lord Lloyd and the Decline of the British Empire* (London, 1987).

81. *Diaries*, II, p. 304.

Amery now exposed Churchill's motives of hoping to ensnare Hoare—thereby impeding the Bill—by delivering the punch line in a loose—very loose, 'vernacular'—translation: 'If I can trip up Sam, the Government is bust.' The House was convulsed with laughter.[82] Churchill was humiliated, but eventually took it in good humour. The incident would not be so significant were it not illustrative of the opposite views held by Amery and Churchill on India. Neither of them would then have predicted that Churchill would select Amery as Secretary of State for India seven years later.

* * *

Amery in the 1930s became increasingly aware of the danger of Germany, a theme which bears examination in relation to the issue of strategic security and the subject of appeasement at All Souls. The phrase 'All Souls and Appeasement' was of course the title of the book written by A.L. Rowse of All Souls. Amery liked Rowse and, when writing in 1933 about the younger Fellows, described him as aggressively left-wing but nevertheless 'a shrewd likeable fellow and much the ablest and most constructive among them.'[83] Rowse for his part held Amery in high esteem and described him as a 'brave man', though one regarded by his political colleagues 'as both a bit of a light-

82. 'The fish swallowed the fly.' Amery MS Diary, 13 June 1934. Amery discusses the episode at length in *My Political Life*, III, pp. 103–04: 'My speech was certainly one of the most successful', Amery continued, ' . . . that I ever delivered . . . [and gave] Winston the best ducking he has had since he first pushed me into Ducker in 1889.' For Hoare's account, Viscount Templewood, *Nine Troubled Years* (London, 1954), p. 98.

83. *Diaries*, II, p. 289. In his diaries Amery was consistently sympathetic towards Rowse. For example Amery wrote in 1947 after the publication of Rowse's *Childhood Reminiscences*: 'Very interesting, and in a way artless, but also with the natural egotism of the man who has made his own way against great difficulties.' Amery MS Diary, 18 October 1947.

weight and also . . . something of a right-wing doctrinaire and curiously independent.'[84] Rowse's book casts a shadow on the 'Milner group' at All Souls. It is not much of a shadow, however, because even in Rowse's own account, the disciples of Milner emerge as so highly individualistic that any notion of them as a collective influence simply evaporates. Robert Brand and Dougal Malcolm in the 1930s went to the College only at very irregular intervals.[85] Another two of the 'Empire builders'—Lionel Curtis and Reginald Coupland—are absolved from the guilt of 'appeasement'.[86] The real villains in Rowse's book are Geoffrey Dawson and two Fellows who were only on the fringe of the 'Milner group', John Simon and Halifax. The hero is Amery. Rowse writes that 'Leo Amery was consistently opposed to appeasement.' This is a simplistic interpretation.

Lloyd George commented in 1919 about the Round Table group that it was 'a very powerful combination— in its own way perhaps the most powerful in the country. Each member of the Group brings to its deliberations certain definite and important qualities, and behind the scenes they have much power and influence.'[87] Amery had long fallen away from the inner circle of the Round Table movement because he dissented from the aim of Imperial

84. A.L. Rowse, *All Souls and Appeasement* (London, 1961; the title of the New York edition is simply *Appeasement*), p. 108.

85. Brand in any case was anti-appeasement, fiercely so. Malcolm held staunch Imperialist views but steered clear of political controversy. He is not mentioned in Rowse's book.

86. Rowse writes perceptively on both Curtis and Coupland: 'It was . . . remarkable that Lionel Curtis should never have been carried away by . . . crazy nonsense about Germany. . . . Coupland was never for a moment wrong on the one issue [appeasement] that mattered more than any other'. *All Souls and Appeasement*, pp. 26 and 108.

87. *Lord Riddell's Intimate Diary of the Peace Conference and After, 1918–1923* (London, 1933), p. 330.

Federation. But Amery himself through his writings was partly responsible for the mystique of the Round Table members as the 'best brains' in the British Empire just as he was indefatigable as a panegyrist of All Souls as an intellectual élite. Amery, Brand, Curtis, Dawson, and Malcolm were identified one way or another with the policy of appeasement in the 1930s because of their association with All Souls. Was there a conspiracy? Since All Souls is, or was, considered by some to be tantamount to a conspiracy, it is perhaps a plausible question, but in fact there was no more agreement among those at All Souls and in the Round Table movement on the 'German question' than on the issue of Imperial Federation. They were all disciples of Lord Milner, their one bond in common, and thus they were known as the 'Milner group' at All Souls. But there is an irony. If they might sniff and protest that their influence was not so great, that neither the Round Table nor All Souls was a conspiracy, they had only themselves to blame. They were the victims of their own propaganda.[88]

Amery unequivocally opposed appeasement that might touch the British Empire.[89] His attitude towards appease-

88. David Watt, 'The Men of the Round Table', *Round Table*, 235 (July 1969).

89. See L.S. Amery, *The German Colonial Claim* (London, 1939), which resulted from his protracted campaign rebutting the German demands for colonial concessions. 'The book was dashed off in a very great hurry over a few week-ends. . . . But it does give, I think, a fairly clear statement of the main issues involved.' (Amery to John Buchan, 15 June 1939, Amery Papers) See Ritchie Ovendale, *'Appeasement' and the English Speaking World: Britain, the United States, the Dominions, and the Policy of 'Appeasement', 1937–1939* (Cardiff, 1975); and Andrew J. Crozier, *Appeasement and Germany's Last Bid for Colonies* (New York, 1988), esp. p. 162, which accurately sums up Amery's position: 'For Amery "economic nationalism" was now a permanent feature of the world economy. Britain sheltered in her empire under the system of imperial preference to secure her trading interests. It was up to Germany to create for herself a similar sheltered market in eastern Europe.'

ment in Europe—even through the Munich crisis in September 1938—was a more complicated matter. He always attempted to take a realist's view of how shifts in world politics might affect British security. Above all he stressed the need to retain British mastery of the eastern Mediterranean.[90] As early as 1936 he warned of the danger of an anti-British alliance of 'Germany, Italy and Japan, the worst conceivable hostile combination from our point of view.'[91] He thought it folly to alienate Japan over Manchuria. After the Italian invasion of Ethiopia, he publicly pledged not to send 'a single Birmingham lad to his death for the sake of Abyssinia'.[92] He did not believe that the ascendancy of Germany in Europe would necessarily lead Germany into conflict with Britain. Here he pursued a dual policy of sympathy and sternness: 'non-encirclement' of Germany yet no return of her former colonies (though at one stage he was prepared to cede a slice of the Cameroons or the Solomon Islands or the New Hebrides 'as a small sweetener' to placate the Germans).[93] He wrote in 1938 that he favoured 'Anglo-Italian rapprochement' to secure the British position in the Mediterranean, and that he was prepared to give Germany 'a freer hand in the East, at any rate as against Russia and in the Baltic States'.

90. See Lawrence R. Pratt, *East of Malta, West of Suez: Britain's Mediterranean Crisis, 1936–1939* (Cambridge, 1975). Amery does not himself figure in this study, but the background is indispensable.

91. Amery to Beaverbrook, 7 November 1936, Beaverbrook Papers C/7; *Diaries*, II, p. 429. On Amery and his outlook on alliances, see Maurice Cowling, *The Impact of Hitler: British Politics and British Policy 1933–1940* (Cambridge, 1975), p. 121.

92. *My Political Life*, III, p. 425.

93. Amery to Neville Chamberlain, 11 November 1937, Amery Papers. Amery's proposed concessions followed the familiar pattern of generosity with other people's property: 'I should not only welcome their [the Germans] getting concessions in Angola but in the Belgian Congo and French Colonies.' Quoted in Rich, *Race and Empire in British Politics*, p. 85.

He deplored the 'blundering and humiliation' over Czech-oslovakia and had 'deep misgiving at the extent to which we have let down the unhappy Czechs', but he did not see the outcome as unfavourable to British security.[94]

Yet rational appeasement could work only if pursued with rational men. As early as 1932 Amery commented on 'Hitler's absurd personality'.[95] In 1934 he read *Mein Kampf* in 'the original unexpurgated German'. 'I found it very interesting and stimulating', Amery noted in his diary. On some points Hitler's writing impressed him by the quality of 'intense sincerity and clear thinking.' On the other hand Amery had no doubt that Hitler was 'quite insane about Jews and Socialists'.[96] In August 1935 Amery met Hitler at Berchtesgaden. Amery, his wife 'B.', and his son Julian were on holiday in the Bavarian Alps, where the goal was to scale the Watzmann, a peak of 9,000 feet with a face of sheer 6,000 feet above the Königssee. Amery's presence in Germany had been reported by the German Ambassador in London. Hitler extended an invitation to visit him. He met Amery wearing 'a plain grey flannel suit' and giving a rather commonplace impression that he might have been an employee in a men's clothing store.[97]

The following excerpt from Amery's diary in August 1935 indicates that he was still keeping an open mind about Hitler. Indeed, on some issues, such as Germany's economic pre-eminence in central Europe, Amery had no objection. He recognized Hitler's 'New Order' as a reasonable response to the economic problems of the Great

94. *Diaries*, II, pp. 520 and 541.
95. Ibid., 283.
96. Ibid., p. 380.
97. *My Political Life*, III, pp. 127–30.

Depression. On the whole Hitler was a 'bigger man' than Amery had expected:

> We talked . . . for over an hour and a half. I did not find the hypnotic charm I had heard of, and no attempt to exercise it, but liked his directness and eagerness to let his hearer know all his mind. Intellectually he has a grip on economic essentials and on many political ones, too, even if it is crude at times and coloured by deep personal prejudice. . . .
>
> We got on well together I think, owing to the fundamental similarity of many of our ideas. But I admit we didn't discuss some controversial subjects like Austria, constitutional liberty, Jews or Colonies.[98]

In retrospect it is startling that Amery could have pushed aside the vital issues, but he was intent on exploring common economic ground. Hitler was a man with whom it still might be possible to do business, provided, as Amery emphasized repeatedly, there would be 'no surrender of Colonial territory'.[99] In the discussions about colonies during the years 1936–37 Amery demonstrated tenacity, as was his wont, in trying to achieve economic agreement that would not impinge on the territorial integrity of the British Empire.

Not until March 1938 did Amery's attitude change, and then it changed radically.[100] The annexation of Austria was the catalyst. Amery now clearly saw the reign of terror that would follow from Hitler's annexations. 'The news of Austria's collapse came to me as a terrible blow', he

98. *Diaries*, II, p. 397.

99. E.g. ibid., p. 444.

100. The passages in *My Political Life*, III, tend to create the impression that Amery was a more staunch opponent of the Nazi regime at an earlier time than he actually was.

wrote privately.[101] In a letter to *The Times* he stated that clearly there could be no more discussion about a 'settlement' with Germany.[102] In the autumn of the same year Amery listened to Hitler's speech at the *Sportspalast* in Berlin during the Munich crisis: 'It was the most horrible thing I have ever heard, more like the snarling of a wild animal than the utterance of a human being. . . . There was something terrifying and obscenely sinister in this outpouring of sheer hatred'.[103]

Notwithstanding Amery's disgust, his mind still balanced the opposing principles of anti-appeasement and pro-appeasement at the time of the Munich crisis and the dismemberment of Czechoslovakia in September 1938. On the one hand, he had always favoured the accommodation of German aims in central Europe. He found himself at odds with Chamberlain not over the appeasement policy itself but over the slapdash way it had been conducted from one crisis to the next, upholding Czech rights one moment and abandoning them the next. Amery was disinclined to protest because he did not believe that the Munich settlement negatively affected the British Empire. Indeed, the British position was indirectly strengthened:

> We may be giving Germany much greater power in Central Europe, but on the other hand our own position becomes psychologically and strategically much simpler. Fundamentally it is a policy which I have always favoured; my difference on this occasion has been not with the policy itself, but for adopting a very different policy up to the last

101. *Diaries*, II, p. 496.
102. *My Political Life*, III, p. 238.
103. Ibid., p. 278.

moment and then abandoning it under panic conditions which are only likely to increase Hitler's arrogance.[104]

On the other hand, Amery's intellect as well as his instinct rebelled against all that Hitler stood for: 'When I think of the outrageous conduct of Germany I cannot help seeing red, and reason tells me that there can be little permanence in a settlement won by sheer threat of violence.'[105] Amery's repugnance towards Hitler as a dangerous and arrogant thug was now definitely in the ascendancy.

It is much to Amery's credit that his insight into Hitler essentially as a gangster triumphed at last over the urge to accommodate Germany so that the British Empire might prosper. The following passage sums up Amery's premonitions—and his faith—at the time of Munich: 'we may find ourselves besieged in Hong Kong, and Singapore, driven out of Egypt and Palestine, with most of London and our chief munition works in ruins. But perhaps the same national character that has got us into this mess will see us through to the end. Anyhow thank God we are not Germany and capable of being led by a man like Hitler.'[106] Amery now had absolutely no doubt about British honour and justice pitted against 'all the powers of darkness, gangsterism, brutality, persecution, mendacity.'[107] Such a Manichaean vision might appear surprising or even naive in view of his earlier outlook, but once Amery decided that war was inevitable his intellect bat-

104. *Diaries*, II, p. 529.
105. Ibid., p. 510.
106. Ibid., p. 518.
107. Ibid., p. 514.

tened down for a primordial struggle to defend the British Isles against a barbarian power.

The urgent need for rearmament brought Amery and Churchill into common cause. They saw eye to eye, as Amery put it, on the disastrous policy of 'famous disarmament' in the 1930s. Amery recalled that the overriding issue of war and peace had linked the two of them as comrades-in-arms since the Boer War: 'So now Winston and I are once more working together in the third war', he wrote as early as 1938.[108] Amery began systematically preparing himself on such questions as home defence and air strategy, economic resources and strategic raw materials, iron ore and oil.[109] He saw himself perhaps as Churchill's co-ordinator of defence or economic policy. He was to be bitterly disappointed, in part because he believed he had Churchill's confidence. At the time of Austria's annexation in March 1938, Churchill stated that Amery was 'the only person' whose judgement had proved consistently sound in the preceding three years.[110] In holding that view, Churchill in part paid tribute to the relentless logic with which Amery criticized the Chamberlain government and pressed for a policy of national unity. In his memoirs Amery depicted himself as an even greater critic of Chamberlain than he was at the time, but Churchill's comment was essentially correct.

On the eve of Britain's declaration of war in September 1939, Amery believed that Chamberlain had neither the

108. Ibid., p. 517.

109. He wrote to Churchill: 'I believe that the shortage of the alloy minerals, chrome, vanadium, manganese, etc., may be as decisive in ending the war as anything else.' Amery to Churchill, 'Private and Personal', 10 October 1939, Amery Papers.

110. *Diaries*, II, p. 499.

personal strength nor the political vision to lead the country. 'For two whole days the wretched Poles had been bombed and massacred', Amery wrote later, but nevertheless Chamberlain seemed intent on allowing Hitler a last opportunity for 'another Munich'.[111] On 2 September Chamberlain made a spiritless speech to the House of Commons. In Amery's description, he explained 'in a flat embarrassed voice' that the details of the ultimatum to Hitler had yet to be set. Chamberlain failed entirely to catch the spirit of the House or the mood of the public. In Amery's view the time had come to end the confusion and disarray of party politics, but unfortunately the leader of the Labour Party, Clement Attlee, was absent and the deputy leader, Arthur Greenwood, rose to respond to Chamberlain. Amery feared that he would merely state the position of the Labour Party. Thus Amery raised his own voice in what became one of his most famous interventions. With words that electrified the House, Amery shouted 'Speak for England'. Chamberlain's head whipped round as if he had been shot.[112]

In 1939 Amery was sixty-five years old and ten years out of office.[113] But he had a reputation as a man of integrity and judgement who had the courage to speak his

111. *My Political Life*, III, p. 324.

112. Donald Cameron Watt, *How War Came: The Immediate Origins of the Second World War, 1938–1939* (New York, 1989), p. 579. Chamberlain wrote to his sister: 'The House of Commons was out of hand, torn with suspicions. . . . Amery [was] . . . the most insulting of all' (p. 593).

113. When Churchill returned to the Admiralty in September 1939, Amery felt that his own talents were being wasted: 'it is absurd that I should not be being made use of today. After all, next to Winston and Hankey, I know more about the conduct of war than any of them [in the War Cabinet], not to speak of my greater knowledge of European affairs and my authority with the Dominions. And if I am just senior to Winston in actual years, I am, I think, a good deal junior in body, and not yet fossilized in mind.' Amery to Dawson, 4 September 1939, Dawson Papers 81.

convictions regardless of consequence. He rose to the occasion of the wartime emergency. In May 1940 he achieved his finest Parliamentary hour by invoking the words of Oliver Cromwell against Neville Chamberlain. The era of Cromwell was one of Amery's favourite historical topics and he knew many quotations by heart. On the morning of 7 May, while preparing for the debate on the German conquest of Norway and the loss of the Norwegian Army, he refreshed his memory on Cromwell's speeches and came upon the 'strong meat' that summarized his own argument. In the debate itself Amery dwelt on the necessity of creating a War Cabinet similar to the Lloyd George War Cabinet with a half dozen men, freed from departmental burdens, sharing the direction of the war (though Amery may not have known it, the example had little attraction to Churchill).[114] Amery quoted Cromwell but held in the back of his mind the most powerful quotation of all. At the end, sensing that his audience was responding attentively and sympathetically, he let go:

I have quoted certain words of Oliver Cromwell. I will quote certain other words. I do it with great reluctance, because I am speaking of those who are old friends and associates of mine, but they are words which, I think, are applicable to the present situation. This is what Cromwell said to the Long Parliament when he thought it was no longer fit to conduct the affairs of the nation:

'You have sat too long here for any good you have been

114. Amery believed, of course, that the war effort should above all be efficiently run, scientifically managed, and characterized by tough decisions. But his approach was not necessarily shared by others. He once told Kingsley Wood, the Secretary of State for Air, that the Black Forest was a principal location of munition storage in Germany and should be bombed. Wood was aghast: 'Are you aware that it is private property? . . . Why, you will be asking me to bomb Essen next!' Neville Thompson, *The Anti-Appeasers* (Oxford, 1971), p. 222.

doing. Depart, I say, and let us have done with you. In the name of God, go!'[115]

Amery's judgement carried weight in Parliament and throughout the country because of his undisputed integrity. The words later used by Lord Wavell, Viceroy of India during the latter part of the war, expressed the public image of Amery from about 1940: 'What a gallant, loyal, straight little man he is'.[116]

115. See *My Political Life*, III, pp. 358–65.

116. Penderel Moon, ed., *Wavell: The Viceroy's Journal* (Oxford, 1973), p. 128.

III

The Second World War, India, and the Clash with Churchill

1940–1945

AT THE APEX OF Amery's career, the events of the Second World War thrust him again into the affairs of India, the British Empire, and the Anglo-American alliance. The controversy about Imperial Preference versus Free Trade continued to play a central part in all his activities, though in his official capacity he dealt mainly with India and Burma. Churchill offered Amery the India Office on 13 May 1940. It would be an understatement to suggest that this was a severe disappointment. It was a stunning and almost humiliating blow. Amery had hoped to serve as Churchill's deputy for defence or as Chancellor of the Exchequer. His sense of patriotism compelled him to consent, but with cool reluctance:

> In accepting I told W[inston] that I felt that he was side tracking me from the real conduct of the war, and . . . I felt that the old gang, and Neville [Chamberlain] in particular, had succeeded in keeping me not only out of the War Cabinet, but out of any real part in things.[1]

Winston wished to keep Leo out of the mainstream business of the war. Yet it was a curious appointment. India was an issue over which they had violently quarrelled. No assignment could have been better calculated to keep them at odds. It eventually had its comic aspects. In Cabinet meetings Amery refused to be bullied by Churchill and yelled back at him. Amery recorded that his colleagues were 'partly shocked and partly delighted that Winston should be spoken to in straight terms'.[2] In their exchanges a lingering schoolboy boisterousness would occasionally come to the surface, but beneath there was a point of real divergence. Amery and Churchill had entirely different conceptions of the British Empire which, in Amery's words, 'have divided us all our lives.'[3]

Amery almost refused the appointment. 'After eleven years of exile from office,' he reflected, he had been offered a second-rate position. On his way home he nearly telephoned to cancel it.[4] 'Public duty' was his own phrase to describe his decision to stick it out. At least, as he

1. *Diaries*, II, p. 617.
2. Ibid., p. 993.
3. Ibid., p. 1021.
4. Ibid., p. 617.

noted, he was now 'inside the fortress' and could help to create a government that would be genuinely committed to 'national efficiency'. Amery was in fact irrepressible. It did not take him long to get over his disappointment and to see that India would be one of the major issues of the war. Nor did he bear a grudge against Churchill. 'He is a real war leader', Amery wrote in late May 1940, 'and one whom it is worth while serving under.'[5]

Amery nevertheless rebelled against Churchill's 'authoritarian instincts'. He wished to see an efficient War Cabinet in which masters of 'groups' of departments could make the intricate wheels of administration move faster —a perfection of the War Cabinet's method of business in the First World War. Churchill had something quite different in mind. 'All I wanted' he wrote later, 'was compliance with my wishes after reasonable discussion.'[6] When Amery argued the merits of refining the Lloyd George system on grounds of national efficiency, Churchill rebuffed him and suspected him of intriguing to change the membership of the Cabinet. Amery in fact not only wished to make the War Cabinet more efficient but also to place in key positions younger men of conspicuous ability such as Harold Macmillan.[7] Thus Amery would have a group of 'young men' comparable to the Milnerites in

5. Ibid., p. 619.

6. Winston S. Churchill, *The Hinge of Fate* (Boston, 1950), p. 89.

7. See the editorial comment in the *Diaries*, II, pp. 600–02. Amery attempted in 1940 to recruit Macmillan for the Colonial Office, a fate that awaited him two years later when he entered, in his own light-hearted phrase, the colonial 'mausoleum'. (Alistair Horne, *Macmillan* [2 vols., London, 1988–89], I, p. 146) Macmillan remained at the Colonial Office only one year, but the experience there shaped his views towards the colonies in ways that were apparent when he became Prime Minister in 1957. Macmillan's daughter, Lady Catherine, married Amery's son, Julian, in 1950.

the First World War. Churchill was exceedingly wary of Amery's behind-the-scenes manoeuvrings.[8]

In truth Amery was not plotting to advance his own position. But Churchill believed that he had an ulterior motive, which had a certain irony. Having helped to bring about the revolution against the Chamberlain government, Amery was now powerless against Churchill. He served at Churchill's pleasure. From the outer ring of the Cabinet, he participated in the debate on the need to keep France in the war and on the danger of a German invasion of Britain. He visited the War Office on a daily basis to study the maps and the progress of battle. His diary contains vivid descriptions of the evacuation of British and French forces from Dunkirk. His contemporary writings convey a sense of the imperishable glory of the RAF during the Battle of Britain as well as the feelings of despair at 'the French Army giving ground both east and west.' 'Poor France', Amery recorded simply and poignantly on 14 June 1940.[9] But these were comments written one step removed from the centre of power.

Amery assumed at first that the principal obstacle in steering India on a 'forward' course would not be Churchill but Lord Linlithgow, the Viceroy. 'Heavy of body and slow of mind, solid as a rock and with almost a rock's lack of awareness', was Jawaharlal Nehru's judgement of Linlithgow.[10] Amery would not have entirely disagreed. Lin-

8. Churchill later remarked to John Colville, his Private Secretary: 'in July 1940 a number of Tories had tried to break up the Government and to engineer the formation of a kind of dictatorial triumvirate consisting of L.G., himself and Bevin. The instigators had been Amery, Harold Macmillan, [Robert] Boothby and P.J. Grigg.' John Colville, *The Fringes of Power* (London, 1985), p. 587.

9. *Diaries*, II, p. 622.

10. Sarvepalli Gopal, *Jawaharlal Nehru* (3 vols., London, 1975–84), I, p. 255.

lithgow had served under him at the Admiralty in 1922. A Scottish peer with long experience in Indian affairs, Linlithgow had chaired the Royal Commission on Agriculture in India (1926–28) and then the Parliamentary committee on Indian constitutional reform (1933–34), which provided the basis for the India Act of 1935. He had been Viceroy since 1936. He had vehemently opposed Churchill over India, as had Amery. But Linlithgow's political instincts were less progressive and certainly more cautious than Amery's. 'L. will I think be a bit startled by my radical views', Amery wrote in his diary in early June 1940.[11]

To understand why Amery's views were regarded as 'radical', it is important to grasp his vision of India's future, which differed sharply from Linlithgow's and fundamentally from Churchill's. Amery believed that India should become fully independent within the Commonwealth and that the Indians themselves should frame their own constitution after the war. India of course did become independent in 1947, and the Indian Constitution of 1950 stands in history as a remarkable chapter in the development of constitutional democracy. The rapid achievement of those great aims makes Amery's views appear today much less radical than they did in 1940. His ideas were then regarded as heretical by Churchill and others on the right wing of the Tory Party who held that India should, one way or another, remain permanently under British sway. Amery too wished to retain the British connection but drew lessons from Canadian and South African history: if the Indians were to decide in favour of the Commonwealth, they must be allowed their own free-

11. Amery MS Diary, 2 June 1940.

dom. Amery's reputation on India has suffered in part merely because he was a member of Churchill's wartime government. Amery was also the victim, as will be seen, of Churchill's brutal and skilful suppression of his initiatives in the summer of 1940. So violent were the initial encounters with Churchill over India that he contemplated resignation.

Amery began optimistically enough. He asked the Viceroy in early June whether various Indian leaders could be invited *'during the war'* to consider India's future *'after the war.'* 'We are always being pressed,' he wrote, 'for a date for inaugurating Dominion Status.' Amery proposed that this issue be decided by a committee composed of 'representative' Indians. As Linlithgow was quick to point out, the very word 'committee' revealed a flaw in the plan. Who would select the committee? 'Men of good will', answered Amery, including Mohandas Karamchand Gandhi. Linlithgow was quite unwilling to admit that Gandhi met that qualification.[12] And so they began to go round and round. Amery's ultimate retort, which he used throughout the war, was that freedom *after the war* should be offered *during* the war and then left to the Indians to decide among themselves how best actually to achieve independence. But, as Amery frequently pointed out, it was highly doubtful whether the Indians could agree

12. Amery to Linlithgow, 2 June 1940; Linlithgow to Amery, 10 June 1940; Amery to Linlithgow, 17 June 1940; Linlithgow to Amery, 20 June 1940; Amery to Linlithgow, 22 June 1940, all secret telegrams in the Amery Papers. Amery was unaware of the extent to which two influential diehards on India, P.J. Grigg and George Lloyd, were in touch with Churchill and reinforced each other's views. 'As you know', Grigg wrote to Churchill in 1940, 'I believe that no settlement in India is possible so long as Gandhi is alive.' Grigg to Churchill 10 November 1940, P.J. Grigg Papers (Churchill College, Cambridge). The George Lloyd Papers are also at Churchill College and they too demonstrate the extent to which Lloyd, Grigg, and Churchill shared uncompromising views on India.

among themselves how to go forward. He thus left himself open to the charge of Machiavellianism, which indeed was an element in his thought. He would not have been dismayed by that accusation. Like other Fellows at All Souls of his generation, he was a student of Machiavelli and believed in a positive sense that rulers should employ justifiable means to maintain strong government. Perhaps just as important, he was able to keep in play various ideas at the same time—such as promising Indian freedom but taking advantage of Indian disarray to prolong British control—which might seem to some to be contradictory but in Amery's mind could be reconciled by choosing the course according to British self-interest. To a greater degree than most of his colleagues, Amery had an academic, indeed Machiavellian, temperament.

Strong government in the case of India meant a strong central government that would be able to hold the country together and mobilize Indian manpower for the war effort. 'My whole conception', Amery wrote to Linlithgow, 'is that of India humming from end to end with activity in munitions and supply production and at the same time with the bustle of men training for active service of one sort or another, the first operation largely paying for the cost of the second.'[13] On the overriding and exuberant point of exploiting Indian resources to win the war, no one dissented. But Amery differed from Linlithgow, and especially Churchill, in wishing to bring about a reconciliation with Gandhi and the leaders of the Congress, above all Nehru and Vallabhbhai Patel. Linlithgow was sceptical whether any concessions short of the British handing over political power, even the ending of the Raj, would per-

13. Amery to Linlithgow, 'Private', 30 May 1940, Linlithgow Papers (India Office Library), MSS Eur. F125/9.

suade Congress leaders to support the British. Churchill was implacably opposed to negotiating with Indian politicians and was hostile even to the idea of India being used for anything other than a reservoir of manpower. Even on the point of Indian economic productivity for the war, Amery and Churchill came into collision. 'Winston . . . hates the idea of Indians producing anything for themselves in the way of defence', Amery noted in his diary.[14]

Amery pressed the Viceroy to seize the opportunity of the moment. After the fall of France, the Congress leaders were in sympathy with Britain. They would respond favourably, Amery believed, to a bold and honest promise to grant Indian independence after the war. To offset Indian distrust, he proposed to offer a definite date (the end of hostilities) and to appoint, straightaway, political leaders to the Viceroy's Executive Council, in other words, to make appointments that would give Indian statesmen real influence in their own national affairs. Linlithgow slowly and reluctantly agreed to Amery's entreaties, which were conveyed by 'private' telegrams (the designation 'private' meant, in effect, unofficial yet secret messages through official channels, which allowed the free exchange of ideas that would not have been possible in formal communications). Amery conducted his business as he had under Baldwin in the 1920s. The present Prime Minister, however, was no Baldwin. When Churchill learned of the exchange of telegrams with the Government of India, he exploded in anger. Having only a few weeks earlier suspected Amery of plotting to change the membership of the War Cabinet, Churchill now accused him of stirring

14. *Diaries*, II, p. 641.

up revolution in India. Did Amery wish to bring about another 'Egypt'?

'You propose', Churchill wrote to Amery in a secret letter on 17 July 1940, 'to create what is virtually an independent India, and to regulate its relations with the Empire by a Treaty. All this is on the Egyptian model.' In an earnest plea to desist, Churchill touched a chord of patriotism that moved Amery profoundly. According to Churchill, it was the worst of all possible times to raise such an issue:

> There is no use in discussing such a change at the present time, and there are no means of thrashing it out in a constitutional way. I hope therefore you will not press me unduly at a time when all our thoughts should be devoted to the defence of the Island and to the victory of our cause.[15]

Amery responded on the same day: 'How can I fail to be moved by an appeal such as you make in your letter?' He offered his assurance that he would not rock the boat in perilous times, but he reminded Churchill that some three and a half decades earlier 'you once blessed self-government in South Africa, which kept South Africa straight in 1914.'[16] The analogy merely made matters worse. In Churchill's mind South Africa and India were not comparable. It may seem out of proportion, but the issue of India in the summer of 1940 stirred Churchill's emotions almost to the same degree as the fall of France.

Churchill directly fired off a telegram asking Linlithgow,

15. Churchill to Amery, 'Secret', 17 July 1940, Amery Papers.
16. Amery to Churchill, 'Personal', 17 July 1940, Amery Papers.

in impassioned yet precise language, whether it was a wise idea to issue 'a new Constitutional declaration' at a time 'when invasion appears imminent, when the life of the Mother-country is obviously at stake. . . ?'[17] An astonished Linlithgow replied that he assumed that Amery's proposal already had the backing of the Cabinet. Amery had in fact qualified his proposals by stating that Cabinet approval would be required. Nevertheless there had been a misunderstanding. Linlithgow would not have moved had he not been goaded and if he had not believed that Amery had the Cabinet behind him.[18] Amery now found himself challenged by Churchill on a matter of principle. Had the Secretary of State for India led the Viceroy to assume that the Cabinet favoured a declaration clarifying Dominion status for India? Had Amery, in Churchill's own words, 'misled the Cabinet'? Churchill threatened to collect and read all of the private correspondence that had passed between Amery and Linlithgow. This was unprecedented interference by a Prime Minister in the affairs of a department. In the judgement of other members of the Cabinet, Halifax above all, Amery had not erred in ventilating ideas with the Viceroy, nor had Linlithgow been deceived. But Churchill did not let the matter rest. He attacked Amery in a meeting of the Cabinet. 'A thoroughly bad morning', Amery wrote in his diary on 25 July 1940. 'Winston began by a tremendous onslaught on me for having misled the Cabinet. . . .'[19] Sir Alexander Cadogan of the

17. Churchill to Linlithgow, 'Secret', 16 July 1940, W.P. (40) 272, CAB 66/10.

18. Linlithgow to Churchill, 'Secret', 18 June 1940, W.P. (40) 272, CAB 66/10.

19. *Diaries*, II, p. 635.

Foreign Office found the confrontation so embarrassing that he left the room.[20]

Amery told Churchill the next day that in normal times he would resign. 'I made clear to him that there could be no question of my having deliberately misled the Cabinet as to Linlithgow's attitude', Amery recorded in his diary. Churchill nevertheless now insisted on seeing all of the private correspondence, some of which contained remarks about his attitude towards India. He read through the telegrams with intense interest. The more he read, the more agitated he became. 'He seemed a good deal perturbed', Amery noted, and went on to record that it was impossible, now more than ever, to reason with Churchill on the subject of India:

> He said he would sooner give up political life at once, or rather go out into the wilderness and fight, than to admit a revolution which meant the end of the Imperial Crown in India . . . Winston said he . . . regarded the whole matter as very serious in that within a few weeks of coming into office I have attempted to initiate a revolutionary policy.[21]

Churchill thus served notice that Amery's position in the Cabinet was precarious. He expected Amery to preside over the Indian war effort, not over the liquidation of the Raj. Part of Churchill's bullying attitude was probably bluff. But his powerful rebuke served the purpose of putting Amery on the defensive. Winston had Leo exactly where he wanted him, in the Cabinet but not in the War

20. David Dilks, ed., *The Diaries of Sir Alexander Cadogan* (New York, 1972 edn.), 25 July 1940, p. 316.

21. *Diaries*, II, pp. 636–37.

Cabinet, in the India Office but not in any position to challenge the existing order.

Amery was momentarily dejected.[22] As a result of the Cabinet discussion on 25 July 1940, Churchill himself undertook to redraft the declaration that Linlithgow and Amery had formulated. Churchill's pen obscured the precision and boldness of Amery's statement. The language now became ponderous and vague yet couched in lofty phrases. India would eventually achieve Dominion status, but the timetable and the method were not specified.[23] After the war the British would assist the Indians in devising a future constitution, but the British Parliament would remain free to judge the matter at the appropriate time. The Viceroy would appoint more Indians to his Executive Council and would create an advisory war council which would also include 'representative' Indians. The Muslims were guaranteed that power in India would not be transferred to their disadvantage. This declaration became known as the 'August Offer' because it was made public on 8 August 1940.[24] In India it was greeted as a caricature of the bureaucratic and muddled thought of the Government of India. The 'offer' seemed almost to be calculated as an insult. 'The whole thing', Nehru re-

22. 'Despondent' was the word he actually used in his diary. Halifax was the only one to give much comfort, but like everyone he found Churchill to be intransigent. 'Winston . . . feels terribly strong[ly]', Halifax wrote to Amery, '[and] although I did my best to explain to him that there was nothing so terribly revolutionary about your ideas, I cannot say I was very successful.' Halifax to Amery, 24 July 1940, Amery Papers.

23. 'So long as we indicate neither date nor method,' Amery had written earlier, 'we remain open to the charge that we are insincere and are merely playing for time.' Memorandum by Amery, 6 July 1940, L/PO/6/105d, India Office Records (India Office Library).

24. See especially Gowher Rivzi, *Linlithgow and India* (London, 1978), chap. 5; and R. J. Moore, *Churchill, Cripps, and India* (Oxford, 1979), chap. 2.

marked, 'is fantastic and absurd and has not even the merit of decent phraseology about it.'[25] It was rejected for different reasons by all parties in India, which was precisely what Churchill wished. The British had made, in his opinion, a jolly good offer, which the Indians had rejected.[26] The onus for failure, Churchill pointed out to the Americans and everyone else interested in India's future, did not rest with the British.

The 'August Offer' of nebulous independence after the war was a victory for Churchill and a setback for Amery. Amery himself despised the language in which it was phrased as well as the studied ambiguity. Despite Churchill's redrafting, it echoed Linlithgow's grandiloquence. Amery detested the Viceroy's 'long-winded' style and 'clumsiness of thought'.[27] In cutting the statement down to size, Churchill had used the prolixity of the draft to disguise his own ideas, or rather the lack of them. There was no mention of Amery's guarantee for equality within the Commonwealth, or the right of Indians to frame their own constitution, or the time when they would achieve independence. But Churchill had accepted some of the substance. Here was a recurrent pattern throughout the rest of the war. Amery would make a clear and spirited proposal. Churchill would reject it. On reconsideration, he would endorse it but with serious modifications that robbed it of much of its original intent. But in Amery's view this was better than nothing. 'We have missed the opportunity for a clear cut general statement and substi-

25. Gopal, *Nehru*, I, p. 266.

26. 'The trouble is', Amery wrote in his diary, 'that Winston . . . just hopes that we can sit back and do nothing indefinitely.' *Diaries*, II, p. 679.

27. 'If ever a man was incapable of stating a case simply in private or public it is he.' Ibid., p. 690.

tuted something rather woolly and lacking in precision', Amery wrote in summary of the 1940 encounter with Churchill, but ' . . . I have got pretty well three quarters of what I wanted and a lot of it in Winston's own language to make him committed to paternity.'[28] The phrase 'three quarters' was an exaggeration, but it reflected Amery's relief that the row was over. 'So ends the storm in the Cabinet teacup'.[29]

Churchill himself wrote to Amery: 'Pray think no more of this incident wh[ich] is now ended satisfactorily to all parties concerned.'[30] For Churchill the matter was closed but not forgotten. Amery's attempt to reconcile Britain and India shortly after accepting office in 1940 made an indelible impression on Churchill's mind. Much later he would refer to Amery as responsible more than anyone else for having 'given away' India.[31] Churchill even kept his file on the 1940 episode and showed it to Anthony Eden in 1953 to demonstrate how Amery, having cast away India, now wished to hang on to the Suez Canal. 'A very strange story', Eden commented.[32] It was an ambiguous remark, but one that could hold true for Churchill's elephantine memory of the way he believed Amery had crossed him on India in the summer of 1940.

* * *

28. Ibid., pp. 637–38.

29. Amery MS Diary. August 1940.

30. Churchill to Amery, 'Private', 3 August 1940, Amery Papers. According to Halifax's biographer, Halifax had managed to convince Churchill that 'Leo was more fool than knave.' Andrew Roberts, 'The Holy Fox': A Biography of Lord Halifax (London, 1991), p. 246.

31. E.g. Amery MS Diary, 16 November 1953.

32. See the correspondence and minute of 18–19 November 1953 in the Avon (Sir Anthony Eden) Papers (University of Birmingham Library), AP 19/1/81.

Amery believed the unity of India to be a transcendent priority. Realistically, however, he had to consider other possibilities. In the 1940s there were three basic solutions to the problem of India: (1) a unified India as embraced by Amery in 1940 and espoused again in refined form by the Cabinet Mission in 1946; 'local option' as suggested by Sir Stafford Cripps in 1942 as the extreme consequence of self-determination; and the partition in 1947 accomplished by Lord Mountbatten. Amery regarded 'local option', or the right of localities and provinces to determine their own future, as the worst possible solution because it would lead to 'balkanization' and fragmentation into ethnic or other units unable to stand on their own either politically or economically. Amery believed that the world was moving in the direction of ever larger political and economic units. He thought that 'local option' was a preposterous concept. In much more serious vein, he held partition to be a retrograde and disastrous step.

There is a delicate irony here. As early as 1940 Amery began to anticipate an eventual transfer of power. Yet he would defer to no one in his desire to preserve the British connection. It was imperative to him that India remain in the Commonwealth. Eventually he was prepared to sacrifice the unity of India to achieve that end, even though he regarded the 'break-up of India, on Ulster and Eire lines . . . [as] a most disastrous solution'.[33] The more he studied the possibility of partition, however, the less catastrophic it appeared. He consciously decided, almost immediately on assuming office, that for military and political reasons the British had to remain on good terms with the

33. Amery to Linlithgow, 'Private', 16 September 1940, Amery Papers.

Muslims. He wrote explicitly of a pro-Muslim British policy. Here as elsewhere there was an element of *realpolitik* in Amery's thought. It was not difficult for him to adjust to the idea that Indian freedom might lead to more than one new member of the Commonwealth. Amery indeed appears as one of the key figures within the British government in the tilt towards a separate Muslim state.[34] If one pursues this proposition to its logical extreme, then Amery has a claim to be one of the fathers of the Pakistani nation, just as three decades earlier during the First World War he participated in decisions that led eventually to the creation of the state of Israel. The irony is that he aimed, above all, to preserve a unified India. But he found it safer to play it both ways.

Amery in fact consistently deplored the idea of a Muslim state. He initially spoke scornfully of the leader of the Muslim League, Mohammad Ali Jinnah, as unworthy of solemn consideration. 'The miserable Jinnah', Amery wrote in September 1940. 'My reading of him is that he is eaten up with vanity and was only prepared to co-operate if he felt that he was to be the shadow behind the throne in the future.'[35] No less preposterous than Jinnah's personality was, in Amery's opinion, the possible composition of a Muslim state:

> The North-Western piece of Pakistan would include a formidable Sikh minority. The North-Eastern part has a Muslim majority so narrow that its setting up as a Muslim state, or part of a wider Muslim state, seems absurd. . . .

34. See e.g. *Diaries*, II, p. 780, where Amery in February 1942 refers to giving 'the Moslems the power to have their Pakistan'.
35. Amery to Linlithgow, 'Private', 30 September 1940, Amery Papers.

> In fact an all out Pakistan scheme seems to me to be the prelude to continuous internal warfare in India.[36]

Disintegration into war, 'break-up' into 'utter disaster'. These phrases occurred whenever Amery wrote about the prospect of a Muslim state. 'Pakistan would mean the beginning of endless civil war in India till the next conqueror from outside came along.'[37] Nevertheless, within a few months, he began to take Jinnah more seriously despite the 'illusion' of Pakistan. As if acknowledging a disagreeable fact, Amery wrote some nine months after assuming office: 'Jinnah and his Pakistanis are beginning to be more of a menace and to have lost all sense of realities.'[38]

If Amery was anti-League, he was even more vehemently anti-Congress. If he detested Jinnah, he also mistrusted Gandhi and especially Nehru. He recognized Congress as the mainstream nationalist movement in India (in contrast to the League, which represented only a small minority of Muslims); but he also saw Nehru as a singular menace who might drive Indian nationalists into rebellion. 'Nehru . . . seems to me the one person determined to push things to extremes.'[39] Amery believed, more accurately, that Gandhi would stand above the conflict between the Congress and the British and that he represented more of a symbolic than an immediate danger. His influence, though negative, would

36. Amery to Linlithgow, 'Private', 16 September 1940, Linlithgow Papers, MSS Eur. F125/9.

37. Amery to Linlithgow, 'Private', 13 December 1940, Linlithgow Papers, MSS Eur. F125/9.

38. Amery to Linlithgow, 'Private', 25 January 1941, Amery Papers.

39. Amery to Linlithgow, 'Private', 23 October 1940, Linlithgow Papers, MSS Eur. F125/9.

not be decisive. In other words, Amery believed Gandhi to be over the hill. Gandhi could not prevent, as Amery had once hoped, the development of a deadly 'triangular duel' between the British, the Congress, and the Muslim League.

The phrase 'triangular duel' might be considered a solecism unless Amery had in mind the British taking on both the Congress and the League, which was indeed what he feared. The idea of the three-sided struggle illuminates his basic concept, which differed from both that of Churchill and Linlithgow, on the one hand, and that of Attlee and Cripps on the other. It is a vital distinction. Amery once expressed his anxiety to Churchill about 'the growing cleavage between Moslem and Hindu.' Churchill responded: 'Oh, but that is all to the good.'[40] Linlithgow too regarded conflict among the three parties as inevitable. Amery did not. He hoped to find a harmony of interests rather than perpetual strife. But his attitude also differed from his Labour colleagues who were, at least in the early part of the war, more sympathetic towards the Congress. Amery believed as a matter of principle that the Congress nationalists should be dealt with on the same footing as other nationalists. 'We are not going to make a deal with Congress behind the back of the minorities.'[41] Attlee and Cripps would have resented any suggestion that they proposed to accommodate the Congress at the expense of others. Yet in the end they did yield to Nehru more than to Jinnah. It was collaboration with Congress that eventually led to the success of Attlee and Mountbatten in 1947. By contrast, the logic of Amery's position in stand-

40. *Diaries*, II, p. 676.

41. Amery to Linlithgow, 'Private', 23 October 1940, Linlithgow Papers, MSS Eur. F125/9.

ing firm against the Congress placed him generally in the camp of Churchill and Linlithgow.

'We are now in the good position', Amery wrote to Churchill in August 1940 after they had patched up their quarrel, 'of being able to say that, if Congress is prepared to play, India can make more rapid progress towards self-government.'[42] Amery disliked the verbosity of the August 1940 statement guaranteeing the position of the Muslims. He would have preferred to be more explicit about the prospect of independence within the Commonwealth. But it was Amery's own ingenuity that had devised the formula enabling the British 'to stand firm on our declared policy.' Amery's position was so balanced and so rational that it could almost be interpreted as a sophisticated version of the old game of divide and rule. The British could nail their colours to the mast knowing that they would not please everyone. The calculation, however, was that Indian divisions would allow British influence to remain predominant. Amery pursued a policy that would have been instantly recognizable to old India hands, many of them long in the grave, as 'masterly inactivity'. The British would be impartial, whether to the Muslim League or to the Hindu Mahasabha on the far right of Indian politics. Here is the essence of Amery's outlook on holding the balance: the Muslims would be assured that they need not fear 'a Hindu Raj'; 'the Hindus, whether of the Mahasabha or Congress brand', would be equally assured that the British were 'not in Jinnah's pocket, and that they [the Congress nationalists] need not fear a Muslim Raj as an alternative to a Hindu Raj.'[43]

42. Amery to Churchill, 16 August 1940, Amery Papers.
43. Amery to Linlithgow, 'Private', 23 October 1940, Linlithgow Papers, MSS Eur. F125/9.

Amery's capacity to hold such fantastic ideas reveals one of his weaknesses. He believed that rational men with similar assumptions about the nature of Indian politics and the 'Hindu mentality' could shape the future, almost as if sitting in committee at All Souls. It would, indeed, be Fellows of All Souls who would provide guidance based on experience elsewhere, notably South Africa. Amery remarked to Lionel Curtis in August 1940:

It is no good our sitting back and saying 'When you [Indians] have agreed, we will think about doing something'. What is needed, of course, is a small band of pioneers who will run about India in the way that you and your friends ran about South Africa in the years before Union, bringing people together in study groups etc.[44]

Expounding similar ideas to other friends, Amery took action. He arranged for Reginald Coupland (who, as has been mentioned, was a Fellow of All Souls and Professor of the History of the British Empire at Oxford) to go to India to write a report on the problem of the constitutional impasse.[45] Amery also pressed on the Viceroy the appointment of a younger Fellow of All Souls, H. V. Hodson, as Reforms Commissioner (constitutional adviser).[46] Amery's circle at All Souls thus became a

44. *Diaries*, II, p. 661.

45. See Reginald Coupland, *The Indian Problem: Report on the Constitutional Problem in India* (Oxford, 1944).

46. Linlithgow acquiesced in the appointment (1941–42), but later wrote for the record that any further All Souls influence might lead 'an innocent [new] Viceroy straight up the garden path!' Minute by Linlithgow on Amery to Linlithgow, Private, 16 September 1942, Linlithgow Papers, MSS Eur. F124/11. Hodson had been editor of the *Round Table* and eventually became editor of the *Sunday Times*. He wrote one of the classic works on India's partition, *The Great Divide* (London, 1969).

brains trust on India, but not with conspicuous success.[47]

Once he regained his equilibrium after his collision with Churchill in 1940, Amery proved to be an efficient and effective Secretary of State. Nothing escaped his attention. He was unrivalled in the mastery of the bureaucracy. He redrafted everything as far as possible in his own language and often with his own pen. In one important case in 1940, Amery modified the Viceroy's policy in a way that had far-reaching consequences. Linlithgow regarded the Congress as the enemy from within. He wished to proscribe the party and all of its members. Membership in the Congress would be regarded as a criminal offence. In Linlithgow's own blunt phrase, there should be 'extinction' of the Congress. 'I feel very strongly', the Viceroy wrote, that the Government of India should issue a declaration which would aim ' . . . to crush the organization as a whole.'[48] The declaration was known as the 'Revolutionary Movements Ordinance'.

Amery believed that banning the Congress would be the height of folly. Why father the revolutionary thought that Indian nationalism possessed the capacity to overthrow the Government of India? Rather than outlawing the party as a whole, he preferred prosecuting individual members. On this point Amery carried the War Cabinet: 'It would give rise to an infinity of trouble if it was intended to make membership of the Congress party a criminal offence.'[49] Nevertheless Amery regarded civil disobedience as disruptive of the war effort and therefore as an

47. Lord Wavell (Linlithgow's successor) wrote to Amery later in the war: 'Coupland's book, which was a careful and scholarly study of the whole problem, was hardly noticed and is treated by nationalists with contempt.' Wavell to Amery, 'Private & Secret', 20 December 1944, Amery Papers.

48. Rizvi, *Linlithgow and India*, p. 163.

49. War Cabinet Minutes, 293 (40) 7, 21 November 1940, CAB 65/10.

activity punishable by political and legal action. Gandhi's followers would be dealt with by the police and in the courts. Gandhi himself would be allowed to fast to death if he wished. On these issues Amery demonstrated a tough, no-nonsense attitude. He did not flinch, as will be seen, from moving against the members of the Congress as whole when he believed them to be guilty of insurrection. Amery had liberal and progressive ideas, but he was willing to put them into cold storage for the critical period at the beginning of the war. He certainly fulfilled his pledge to Churchill not to stir up the issue of possible independence. On general issues of the war, he supported Churchill to the hilt. 'We may differ on India', he wrote to Churchill in November 1941, 'but I yield to none in my admiration for what you have done and are doing in the wider field, and am only anxious to give you all the help in my power.'[50]

* * *

If one event more than any other represented a landmark in the war, it was to Amery the fall of Singapore in February 1942. The Japanese onslaught brought one of the great defeats in British military history and caused Amery, even Churchill, to ponder the fate of India. The reason was simply stated by an American observer of the British predicament: 'The only way to get the people of India to fight . . . [is] to get them to fight for India.[51] Would India resist further Japanese aggression? The British now fought against a deadly combination, which Amery had at-

50. Amery to Churchill, 29 November 1941, Amery Papers.

51. Adolf Berle (Assistant Secretary of State), quoted in Moore, *Churchill, Cripps, and India*, p. 62.

tempted to prevent, that of Japan, Italy, and Germany. But there was an even greater danger. In August 1941 the British, in Amery's view, had endorsed the war aims of the United States by acquiescing in the Atlantic Charter. In a moment of peril, Churchill had committed Britain, again according to Amery, to a postwar order at variance with British economic and political self-interest.[52] This famous declaration by Churchill and Roosevelt not only proclaimed general aims of freedom and democracy but also established the goal of lowering tariff barriers, thus posing a threat to Amery's political credo of Imperial Preference. Over the long haul the United States might prove a mortal enemy of the British Empire.

If Amery believed that Churchill was unbalanced on the subject of India, some of Amery's critics believed that he was fanatical on the issue of Imperial Preference and the challenge, in the phrase he often used, of 'American *Lebensraum*'. So passionately did Amery feel about the American drive to undermine the British economic system that he did not hesitate to say even during the war that he preferred Hitler's 'New Economic Order' to the 'lunatic proposals' made by Roosevelt's Secretary of State, Cordell Hull. The following passage, taken from a letter written by Amery to J. C. Smuts of South Africa, is representative:

I think we make a great mistake if we under-rate the attractiveness of Hitler's 'New Order' for most of Europe. The conception of Europe as a single economic system

52. 'We shall no doubt pay dearly in the end for all this fluffy flapdoodle', Amery wrote on 14 August 1941. *Diaries*, II, p. 710. For insight into Amery's economic views during the war, see David Reynolds, *The Creation of the Anglo-American Alliance 1937–1941* (Chapel Hill, N.C., 1982), pp. 270–71.

... does offer a great deal, even if these advantages have to be paid for by a measure of economic as well as political servitude to Germany. ...

If all we have to offer is a return to the pre-war anarchy in which every European nation has to fight its way in the world as a unit ... then I think many of them would sooner prefer economic stability under Hitler.[53]

Amery viewed the Atlantic Charter and Article VII of the Mutual Aid Agreement of 1942 (designed to eliminate Imperial Preference) as a brazen attempt by the United States to force Britain at one stroke to abolish the sterling area in favour of Free Trade, and thereby to establish economic hegemony over Britain.[54] 'The great danger after the war will be that the United States will come in with as crude and impossible ideas of world economic organisation as it did about world political organisation after the last war.' He held that the American attempt to break up the sterling area and preference agreements was unremitting, hostile, and cold-blooded. He had an un-wavering antipathy towards American power. He wrote later on in the war: 'I only wish sometimes I were in a free position to say what I think about the Atlantic Charter and all the other tripe which is being talked now, exactly like the tripe talked to please President Wilson.'[55]

The villains in Amery's book were Cordell Hull, an 'ideologue' with distinctly 'nineteenth-century' ideas about Free Trade, and Sumner Welles, the Under Secretary of State, who combined a commitment to Free

53. *Diaries*, II, pp. 702–03.

54. For the economics of the wartime proposals, see Richard N. Gardner, *Sterling-Dollar Diplomacy* (Oxford, 1956), pp. 150–60 and chap. XVII; and for British discussions, see Christopher Throne, *Allies of a Kind* (London, 1978), p. 137 *et passim*.

55. *Diaries*, II, p. 826.

Trade in equal measure with a determination to promote 'independence' in the European colonial empires.
Amery's opinions of these redoubtable American statesmen were a caricature, but he accurately detected the
underlying belief of both Hull and Welles that the world
would be a better place if there were fewer tariff barriers
and fewer empires. Free Trade and self-interest for the
Americans interlocked, much as had been the case for the
British in the nineteenth century.[56] Since Churchill himself
was still at heart a Free Trader, he did not defend the
protectionist cause with anything near the ferocity that
Amery believed to be necessary: 'Winston certainly will
be no help: he isn't even capable of understanding what
is at issue.[57] Fortunately for Amery, Roosevelt was not
as 'fanatic' as Hull and Welles. Roosevelt proved willing
to postpone discussion on economic issues. 'A fad of Cordell Hull's' was the phrase Amery recorded in his diary
about the way in which the President described Hull's
obsession with Free Trade.[58] On the issue of ending the
colonial Empire, however, Roosevelt was not so easily
deflected.

The Atlantic Charter embraced the principle of self-
determination. Churchill intended it to apply to the European nations conquered by the Nazis. Amery, however,
immediately saw that the idea would be seized upon by
Asian and other nationalists. Once encouraged, where
would they stop? What would become of the British Empire? Would it be handed over to a new international
organization committed to the liquidation of the European

56. See John Gallagher and Ronald Robinson, 'The Imperialism of Free
Trade', *Economic History Review*, Second Series, VI, 1 (1953).

57. Amery MS Diary, 9 August 1941.

58. Amery MS Diary, 17 January 1942.

empires? Such questions troubled Amery. Had the British lost the will to govern?

> This appalling defeatism about our mission in the world horrifies me. The place seems full of people who really think that the solution of everything after the war is to hand it over to the Americans, or the Chinese, or the Russians, or some mixed committee of all of them. . . .
>
> Just before Cabinet I saw a . . . telegram from Chiang Kai-Shek to Roosevelt urging him to interfere in India; I sped it on its way to Winston with a strong telegram urging Winston to tell Roosevelt to tell the Generalissimo to mind his own business.[59]

'Tripe' was the word Amery reiterated to sum up his opinion about the value of the phrase 'national self-determination'.

Amery and Churchill held identical views on not allowing the Americans, or anyone else, to meddle in the affairs of the British Empire. Amery prepared a statement for Churchill proclaiming at some length that the self-determination clause of the Atlantic Charter (Article III) had nothing to do with India or the colonial Empire. Amery had no doubt that Churchill would accept it. Instead Churchill made his own declaration without consulting his Secretary of State for India. Churchill 'cut it down to a sentence and greatly upset India'. What Churchill said, in effect, was that the Atlantic Charter applied to Europe, not to India, Burma, or the colonies, and that the British had their own pledges on self-government and freedom. Amery acknowledged that this was an 'ingenious . . . side-stepping [of] the matter by referring to past

59. Amery MS Diary, 12 August 1942.

declarations.'[60] The 'past declarations', however, did not exist in any systematic form. The Colonial Office as well as the India Office now had to search for the precedents that the Prime Minister had openly proclaimed.[61] Churchill drew inspiration without sensing the need to confer with his colleagues. To Amery it was an alarming procedure. 'He never consults me if he can help it', Amery later lamented.[62]

Amery immediately found himself embroiled with a delegation of Burmese leaders who were visiting London on a goodwill mission in October 1941. Burma was part of his official domain. He once described it as a country 'conveniently administered as part of an autocratically governed Indian Empire'.[63] The Burmese Premier, U Saw, tried to make Amery see the writing on the wall: the era of autocracy was dead. The Burmese demanded immediate self-government and invoked Article III of the Atlantic Charter to strengthen their claim. They insisted upon independence within the British Commonwealth as soon as possible. They would not wait for the end of the war. Amery found these demands tedious. At first he did not take U Saw seriously. 'His chief interests in life are drink [and] pretty ladies'.[64] Though U Saw 'swelled visibly round the middle' during his visit, Amery nevertheless

60. *Diaries*, II, pp. 713–14.

61. These points are discussed at length in Louis, *Imperialism at Bay*, chap. 6, 'Article III of the Atlantic Charter—Self-Determination', e.g. Harold Macmillan: 'I do not think the P.M. can have realised the true nakedness of the land when he made the statement.' (p. 132) On reading the evidence in the Amery Papers, I now tend to agree with David Reynolds on a specific point about Churchill: 'he simply said that the Atlantic Charter was a separate topic from decolonization . . . it was a masterful piece of Whitehall obfuscation.' *Creation of the Anglo-American Alliance*, p. 364.

62. Amery MS Diary, 31 December 1941.

63. Amery, *My Political Life*, III, p. 109.

64. Amery MS Diary, 11 October 1941.

had to acknowledge that the Burmese leader tenaciously pursued his political goals. He doggedly insisted, in Amery's words, on sweeping away 'every vestige' of British control. Amery stuck to a promise of independence after the war. The Burmese delegation left London in a disgruntled mood. Amery was convinced that U Saw would try to establish himself as a dictator and, after the attack on Pearl Harbor, feared that he might 'proclaim a Quisling Government of Burma.'[65] These were disturbing thoughts. If the Burmese were capable of such 'treachery', could the Indians be far behind?

Amery slept uneasily, fearing the worst. His nightmares included scenes of a 'Pétainist' India under Gandhi and, even worse, of a rebellion that would require British repression no less forcible than during the Mutiny of 1857. Yet he possessed a basic confidence in India. His faith distinguished him from most of his colleagues, especially from the Viceroy. Linlithgow believed that Burma and India were so alien in 'race, history and religion' that they remained part of the British Empire only because the Indians regarded the British as tantamount to conquerors.[66] 'Not altogether to my liking', was Amery's reaction to Linlithgow's reflections on the relationship between subjects and rulers.[67] Linlithgow's views on India in fact represented the opposite of Amery's political principles. Amery held that the British were in India because they had a mission. The British might not be universally liked, but they were respected. Indians of all political and religious persuasions ultimately would recognize the immense

65. *Diaries*, II, p. 761.

66. Linlithgow to Amery, 21 January 1942, Nicholas Mansergh and others, eds., *The Transfer of Power 1942–47* (12 vols., London, 1970—83), I, p. 49.

67. *Diaries*, II, p. 728.

benefits of British rule. British justice and liberty as well as a sense of fair play had been planted in a unified India. The vast majority of Indians already acknowledged the advantages of peace and economic progress within the 'steel frame' provided by the British. Amery calculated that India would hold to the British side, partly because of genuine loyalty. Nevertheless he did not rule out the possibility of rebellion. He prepared himself mentally for the prospect of insurrection. It might be best, Amery mused, 'to go back more to the spirit of Mutiny days and revive British Rule in its most direct and, if necessary, ruthless form.'[68]

With the Japanese advancing towards India, Churchill decided that he himself should fly out to steady the situation. He responded, Amery observed, not merely to the combined pressure of Roosevelt and Chiang Kai-shek, both of whom insisted that India should be offered at least a measure of freedom to keep her in the war. Churchill also faced the criticism of Attlee, who was outraged at the 'crude imperialism' of the Viceroy. Attlee and other Labour leaders believed that inspired leadership in both Delhi and London would be necessary to rally the Indians. Churchill rose to the occasion. He was capable of swings of mood and outlook as well as political invention. 'He really is an extraordinary creature', Amery wrote, 'both in methods and in the extraordinary gaps in his knowledge and outlook all coupled with elements of real genius.'[69] With remarkable political agility and ebullience of spirit, Churchill prepared the way for an agreement with the leaders of the Congress whom he usually denounced as part of the 'Hindoo Priesthood'. But the plan to fly to

68. Amery MS Diary, 17 February 1942.
69. Amery MS Diary, 11 February 1942.

India, to Amery's relief, became transformed into a plan to make a broadcast to India. The broadcast in turn gave way to a mission led by a high-ranking Labour member of the British Cabinet to negotiate with the Indian leaders. To Amery's surprise, Churchill agreed with alacrity to the choice of Sir Stafford Cripps, who had joined the War Cabinet on 12 February 1942 after his return from serving in Moscow as Ambassador. The key to what ensued was recorded in Amery's diary at the outset of these developments: Churchill believed that 'it wouldn't matter very much if the scheme fell through.'[70]

Amery followed the twists and turns of Churchill's enthusiasms at first hand. Linlithgow felt cut out. 'I am . . . really cross with you all over this business', he wrote to Amery, 'and I do again beg of you to see to it that I should be in some measure cushioned by you and your Office from the full impact of these explosions in the Prime Minister's mind.'[71] The Viceroy referred to the aborted plan for Churchill to fly to India and the abandoned idea of a broadcast. Amery now had to warn Linlithgow that Cripps was on his way to India. 'Take strongest peg [of brandy] you can before continuing', Amery began the message. Cripps, who possessed one of the most powerful intellects in the Labour Party, indeed one of the keenest legal minds in Britain, would descend on Delhi to discuss the future of India with leaders of the Congress. By telegrams and letters to the Viceroy, Amery began to explain that the adversaries on the left were being given rope to hang themselves. There was an unmistakable logic of *realpolitik* implicit in Amery's messages to both Churchill and Lin-

70. Amery MS Diary, 6 February 1942.

71. Linlithgow to Amery, 'Private and Confidential', 13 February 1942, Amery Papers.

lithgow, neither of whom needed to read between the lines. It might be possible, Amery wrote to Churchill, to come up with an offer that would 'satisfy Moslems and just possibly some of Congress, as well as Americans and the Left Wing here.' In other words, the 'Cripps Offer' would have a definite propaganda value. 'What we have been up against all the time', Amery wrote to the Viceroy, 'is the hope on the part of Congress that its influence with the members of the Left Wing here and in America would push us into going back on the pledge of 1940', the essence of which to Amery was the conciliation of the Muslims. The Congress nationalists would be told that the British would not renege on their commitment to minorities— and 'by someone whom they regard as not unsympathetic,' in other words, Cripps.[72]

It would be a mistake to place too much emphasis on Amery's part in the Cripps mission. On the other hand it would be equally mistaken to portray him, as has Professor W. H. Morris-Jones, as 'baffled and blown about by the storm of policy battlefields.'[73] It is true that on this occasion Amery responded to events more than he shaped them. He sided with Churchill, reasoned with Cripps, and placated Linlithgow. From Amery's own diary it is clear that the principal figures in the struggle for the control of policy were Churchill the diehard Tory on India, Cripps the Labour envoy, and Linlithgow the embattled Viceroy. Nevertheless Amery played an important part as conciliator and, at a different level, as the statesman who established the continuity in British policy.

72. Amery to Linlithgow, 10 March 1942, in Mansergh, ed., *Transfer of Power*, I, pp. 401–02.

73. W.H. Morris-Jones in the *Political Quarterly*, 44, (January–March 1973), p. 94.

This was a game being played for highest political stakes. One of the members of the Cripps mission said to Amery's friend Reginald Coupland that 'if he [Cripps] brought this settlement off, Cripps would certainly replace Winston.'[74] When Cripps joined the War Cabinet in early 1942, he was the leader of the House of Commons. He seemed to be riding the crest of a wave that many people believed or hoped to be the current of the future. The military reversals in the Far East came as a profound shock to the entire nation. On the issue of India, Cripps represented the hope of bringing the Hindus united with the Muslims into the war against the Japanese. As a Socialist he stood for equality in India as throughout the world. He was committed to the cause of Indian freedom. He seemed to offer an alternative to the 'crude imperialism', to repeat Attlee's phrase, of Churchill and Linlithgow. In short Cripps held out the hope of Indian freedom and unity, or, at the minimum, progress towards those goals despite the wartime crisis. He also intended to replace Linlithgow with a Viceroy willing to accommodate those aims. The person of the Viceroy would become a purely constitutional figure analogous to the King of England. The Viceroy's Executive Council would be 'Indianized' in its entirety. The Congress and Muslim League would, he hoped, co-operate in helping to form a truly 'national' government. That Cripps had a good chance of pulling all of this off makes the story all the more fascinating, especially from Amery's point of view. Amery did not quite know how to deal with this champion of socialism and Indian nationalism who was, at the same time, a vegetarian. 'We must have a really good talk before you leave',

74. Moore, *Churchill, Cripps, and India*, p. 82.

Amery wrote to Cripps in early March 1942. 'Would you and Lady Cripps dine quietly with us on Tuesday or Wednesday at 7.45? Do you include fish and eggs in your diet (when procurable!) or are you a vegetarian of the straiter sect?'[75]

While Amery and Cripps austerely dined, Linlithgow braced himself for a disagreeable visit. Cripps had long-standing connections with the Congress leaders, especially Nehru, as well as contacts with British missionaries in India that stretched back into the interwar period.[76] Linlithgow, however, regarded Cripps as a dilettante in Indian politics. In 1942 Linlithgow was himself a powerful figure who was usually underestimated by his British colleagues. His Indian expertise encompassed all areas of government and his general knowledge was capacious. He was the godfather of the 1935 Act. He had been Viceroy for four years—the whole of a normal term. He moved slowly but he was industrious. From the British angle he knew more about Indian politics than perhaps anyone else. He regarded the Cripps mission as undermining his own position by taking the long-term affairs of the Government of India virtually out of his hands. He did not think that the Cripps plan of offering independence after the war was sound, or that the idea of a 'national government' would be either workable or acceptable to the various Indian parties. Nevertheless the Viceroy decided to stand back, let Cripps operate by himself, and see what happened. Linlithgow made it clear to Amery, in a ponderous sort of way, that the responsibility for interpreting the outcome of the mission remained the Viceroy's alone.

75. Amery to Cripps, 9 March 1942, in Mansergh, ed., *Transfer of Power*, I, p. 390.

76. See Moore, *Churchill, Cripps, and India*, chap. 1.

Amery found himself at the vortex of powerful forces which, he had to confess to Linlithgow, he could moderate but not control. Amery was, however, responsible for one vital element in Cripps's brief which was vital not merely to the mission in 1942 but to the partition of India itself. It was Amery who was responsible for the 'local option' clause that gave the Muslims the right to secede. Amery's own diary is explicit on the way in which he pressed on Cripps and others the principle that a 'dissident province' might be allowed to stand on its own or 'stand out' and not be forced to remain part of a unified India against its will. 'Dissident province' was Amery's veiled phrase to indicate the possibility of Pakistan. He used indirect words and phrases because he did not wish to use the word 'Pakistan' itself. Indeed he hoped that, by driving the principle of self-determination to its logical extreme, Jinnah would be flushed out into the open and would be forced to recognize the absurdity of 'balkanization' or the fragmention of India into ethnic and religious parts.[77] On the other hand, Amery wanted to secure Muslim support by offering them, in effect, Pakistan. Here are some of the crucial passages in Amery's diary:

> Cripps has readily accepted my view that we must make it clear that a dissident province can stand out but not prevent the others framing a constitution. . . . (26 February 1942)
> I was glad to find Cripps and the rest of them prepared to accept my view . . . that any province which disliked the new constitution could stand out. This gives the Moslems the power to have their Pakistan if Congress is not prepared to meet them, but on the other hand does not

77. For analysis on this point, see Ayesha Jalal, *The Sole Spokesman: Jinnah, the Muslim League and the Demand for Pakistan* (Cambridge, 1985), p. 76.

hold the rest of India up indefinitely. . . . (27 February 1942)[78]

The price was high, but Amery was prepared to pay for Muslim support by conceding the theoretical possibility of Pakistan. His attitude is comprehensible because he thought the odds against Jinnah were too great ever to see the birth of a separate Muslim state.[79]

Amery's diary contains scathing references to Churchill's failure to understand the issues. Some of the entries for early 1942 might well have been written ten years later, when Churchill did occasionally lapse into dotage. In reflecting on the debate on the terms of reference for the Cripps mission, Amery wrote:

What really killed the whole discussion was Winston's complete inability to grasp even the most elementary points in the discussion. After one had spent ages explaining the effect of enabling a province to stand out he still harked back to the iniquity of any body on which there was a Congress majority, as if a majority mattered in such a case.

He seems quite incapable of listening or taking in even the simplest point but goes off at a tangent on a word and then rambles on inconsecutively. For the first time I began to feel not merely that he is unbusinesslike but that he is overtired and really losing his grip altogether.

Certainly a complete outsider coming to that meeting and knowing nothing of his reputation would have thought him a rather amusing but quite gaga old gentleman who could not understand what people were talking about.[80]

78. *Diaries*, II, pp. 779–80.

79. E.g. 'Most of the Hindus will set up a howl of protest against the thought of dividing Mother India.' Amery MS Diary, 4 March 1942.

80. Amery MS Diary, 26 February 1942.

Amery concluded eventually that Churchill's confused response did not represent failing faculties as much as it did clashing emotions. It perturbed Churchill to yield on India for the sake of appeasing the United States and the British Left: 'Winston . . . hated the idea of giving up all his most deeply ingrained prejudices merely to secure more American, Chinese, and Left Wing support. He was undergoing all the conflicting emotions of a virtuous maiden selling herself for really handy ready money.'[81]

Cripps came close to achieving a master political stroke that would have altered the course of Indian and British history. In the light of the voluminous documentation, it must be said that Amery was slow in recognizing Cripps's intent (or perhaps that Cripps moved so adeptly at high levels of ambiguity that Amery and others failed to see the implications until late in the game). Amery had acquiesced in the mission initially because he believed that Cripps's position on the Left would make it 'easier for him to carry through what is essentially a pro-Moslem and reasonably Conservative policy'.[82] Cripps arrived in India in late March 1942, however, to work towards the entirely different aim of 'Indianizing' all of the Viceroy's Executive, of replacing the Viceroy himself by a figure who would hold a position comparable to a constitutional monarch, and of creating an Indian 'national government'. By directly negotiating with Nehru and other leaders of the Congress, and by securing the support of the representative of the United States in India (Colonel Louis A.

81. *Diaries*, II, p. 783. Amery continued later in similar vein: 'Both from the point of view of trying to grasp the problem to which he has given so little thought, and from that of the pain of abandoning his old diehard position, the whole thing has been a tremendous strain upon him.' Amery MS Diary, 8 March 1942.

82. Amery MS Diary, 8 March 1942.

Johnson), Cripps moved forward, briefly, without the knowledge of Linlithgow, Amery, or Churchill. Amery's moment of truth occurred on Easter Sunday 1942 when he at last saw the magnitude of Cripps's collaboration with the Congress leaders, who not merely wished to have control over military command but even more: 'Congress is really only putting this [defence issue] forward as part of their general demand that the whole government of India should be handed over to them here and now.'[83]

Amery was appalled at Cripps's audacity. The British would secure the collaboration of the Congress nationalists for the duration of the war, but at what price? Cripps's answer in the end was unequivocal: there should be a substantial transfer of power, which was long overdue. Amery himself thought it desirable to allow the Indians a greater voice in the war, but not in a way that would challenge British control over internal security or over economic, military, and foreign affairs. Least of all did he wish any increase in American influence. Cripps was thus moving in the opposite direction as he attempted to create an alliance between an Indian 'national government' and the United States.[84] He challenged the very basis of the existing order. 'Quite impossible', Amery noted in his diary on 10 April 1942. 'I hastily drafted . . . a telegram explaining this in the most forcible language.'[85]

In Amery's view, Cripps had gone far beyond his in-

83. *Diaries*, II, p. 790.

84. Roosevelt sympathized with Cripps's aims but before he could effectively intervene Cripps was already on the verge of departing from Delhi. See Moore, *Churchill, Cripps, and India*, p. 130. 'I do hope', Amery wrote later to Churchill', 'you will make it quite clear to the President that his people must keep off the grass.' Quoted in Martin Gilbert, *Road to Victory: Winston S. Churchill 1941–1945* (London, 1986), p. 343.

85. *Diaries*, II, p. 793.

structions. Cripps encouraged the Congress leaders to believe 'that all departments apparently except internal affairs were to be handed over to Indian politicians.' What Amery had in mind, in contrast, was to prove sincerity of intent, not to transfer power:

> Cripps seems to have got entirely away from our original standpoint, which was to make our sincerity as to the future absolutely manifest and in the light of that to invite Indians to come and serve on the existing constitutional basis during the war but not in any way to accept . . . a national government of politicians responsible to nobody in particular and able to override the Viceroy. . . .[86]

All of this complicated business occurred in a period of weeks. The Cripps mission technically came to stalemate on the defence issue; but, to Amery's great relief, it finally collapsed on general grounds which suggested, to the British and American public, nationalist intransigence. For Amery it was a close shave. Had the Indians accepted Cripps's proposals, and had the United States been allowed the time to endorse them, it would have been difficult if not impossible to have refused the substance of a 'national government'. 'I . . . feel like someone who has proposed for family or financial reasons to a particularly unprepossessing damsel', Amery wrote in his diary, 'and finds himself lucky enough to be rejected.'[87]

With more brutality and with more of a sense for the jugular, Churchill responded in the same way as Amery.

86. Amery MS Diary, 10 April 1942. For the American side of the story, see especially M. S. Venkataramani and B.K. Shrivastava, *Quit India: The American Response to the 1942 Struggle* (New Delhi, 1979); and Gary R. Hess, *America Encounters India, 1941–1947* (Baltimore, 1971).

87. *Diaries*, II, p. 794.

Learning from Linlithgow that Cripps wanted to change the constitutional status of the Viceroy and to form a 'national government', Churchill moved quickly and decisively to undermine the envoy's position. At this level Churchill and Linlithgow were the principal players, not Amery. Amery was nevertheless vital to the outcome. He put the full weight of the India Office as well as his personal powers of persuasion on Churchill's side. He tenaciously argued that the British had been willing to make immediate political concessions (which admittedly fell far short of Cripps's proposals), thereby giving substance to the long-term promise of independence. He heaved an immense sigh of relief when the Indians themselves rejected the overture. Nevertheless the failure of the Cripps mission had good propaganda value, which Churchill and Amery had foreseen from the outset. To most of the rest of the world, above all to those in the United States, the British had made a reasonable offer which the Indians had scornfully dismissed. With the Cripps chapter closed, Amery wrote, 'we can now go ahead with the war with a clear conscience.'[88]

* * *

From 1942 onwards Amery's involvement in the war can be related more briefly because the general outlines are well established. His quarrel with Churchill over Indian independence approached, in Amery's own phrase, that of a blood feud. A note of alarm, or at least surprise, entered Amery's diary whenever Churchill seemed to be in agreement with him. In the aftermath of the Cripps mission, Amery wrote that Churchill 'now looks upon me

88. Amery MS Diary, 11 April 1942.

as a steady and supporting influence and not as a dangerous innovator!'[89] The fragile rapport lasted through the summer of 1942 when the Cabinet and Viceroy in August moved decisively against the Congress.

Here it is necessary to disentangle British conviction from reality. Amery and others attributed to Gandhi a more disciplined control over the population at large than he actually possessed while the British also exaggerated the pro-Japanese sentiment of the Congress leaders. Amery believed that Gandhi would welcome a Japanese puppet regime in the place of the British Raj. His interpretation did Gandhi an injustice. Gandhi's views were at once more complex and subtle, and less clear-cut, than Amery imagined. The main thrust of Gandhi's thought is now easily discernible even though it seemed confused to contemporary observers. He had no wish to substitute one imperialist power for another. To deal with the Japanese, it would first be necessary to get rid of the British. In the summer of 1942 nationalist sentiment ran high. The fiasco of the Cripps mission seemed to prove that the British aimed to stay in India indefinitely, as indeed was Churchill's intent. Congress prepared to resist. When Amery received police evidence on 13 July 1942 of an impending nationalist revolt, he wrote to Churchill on the need to strike immediately:

Twice armed is he that has his quarrel just;
But thrice armed he who gets his blow in fust.[90]

89. Amery to Linlithgow, 'Private', 10 June 1942, Linlithgow Papers, MSS. Eur. F. 125/11.

90. Amery to Churchill, 13 July 1942, in Mansergh, ed., *Transfer of Power*, II, p. 376. For discussion of Amery and Gandhi in 1942, see Gyanendra Pandey, ed., *The Indian Nation in 1942* (Calcutta, 1988), p. 124.

Gandhi, Nehru, and other Congress leaders were arrested on Sunday, 9 August 1942. During the actual crisis, when railway lines and communications were severed in eastern India in the province of Bihar, Amery orchestrated the Cabinet decisions to clamp down on the insurrection. The Viceroy effectively crushed the revolt. The prompt action, in Amery's judgement, averted a rebellion that threatened to be as grave as the great Mutiny of 1857. The 'Quit India' movement was as much a popular uprising as it was a planned revolt, but Amery saw in the events of 1942 the malevolent genius of Gandhi, whose primary motive was opportunist and anti-British: 'Gandhi's actions all through March 1942 and the subsequent months were dictated by the conviction that we were down and out, and the hope that we might be either persuaded or sabotaged out of India. . . .'[91]

Amery consistently denigrated Gandhi and questioned his moral stature. His views were in line with the later judgement of Lord Wavell, Viceroy from 1943, who once wrote that Gandhi was 70 per cent astute politician, 15 per cent saint, and 15 per cent charlatan.[92] Amery's ideas also bore similarity, in a less sophisticated but equally robust manner, to the interpretation put forward systematically by (Sir) Penderel Moon in *Gandhi and Modern India*.[93] Amery, like Moon later, thought the mystical nature of Gandhi's anti-imperialist vision and the probable realities of a liberated India to be irrecconciable. On this score Amery's views, though hardly original, were certainly representative of British thought:

91. *Diaries*, II, p. 877.
92. Moon, ed., *Wavell: The Viceroy's Journal*, p. 461.
93. Penderel Moon, *Gandhi and Modern India* (New York, 1969).

What I have never been able to discover myself is why he is so universally accepted as a great man even by those who think his politics unpracticable. I should have thought he was a very woolly pacifist, simple, a life preacher with no ideas of any particular distinction who has combined a reputation for holiness most successfully with a political dictatorship exercised in a wrecking and negative sense.

Gandhi seems to be an astute politician who has assumed mysticism for political purposes and may end by being forgotten as a mischievous politician and only remembered as a real saint.[94]

Amery thus had no use at all for Gandhi as a politician and believed that his religious and philosophical thought was somewhat bogus—he was merely a 'holy man'. When he decided 'to fast to capacity' by consuming nothing but lime juice and water for twenty-one days in early 1943, Amery was prepared to let him starve himself to death.[95]

Amery's attitude towards Gandhi was not far removed from Churchill's. But on economic issues Amery and Churchill remained poles apart. 'I confess I find myself getting very impatient when he talks really ignorant nonsense', Amery recorded after a Cabinet discussion on sterling balances in September 1942.[96] The war had converted India from Britain's debtor to creditor. 'Sterling balances', Amery explained to Churchill in as basic a way as possible, were the sums of money owed to India 'for value received', including supplies to the Middle East as well as Indian troops fighting outside India. Churchill refused to acknowledge the point. He would, in Amery's phrase, 'bur-

94. *Diaries*, II, p. 875.

95. E.g. Amery MS Diary, 9 February 1943. When Gandhi was released in May 1944 on grounds of ill health, Amery noted, 'the old rascal will be allowed out . . . and I trust may fade out before long.' *Diaries*, II, p. 982.

96. Ibid., p. 833.

ble away endlessly' that it was 'monstrous' to pay the Indians for the privilege of expelling the British. Churchill's line in fact had nothing to do with the economic case. 'The rest of the Cabinet look down their noses or smile when he is not looking but don't do very much to help', Amery lamented.[97]

It is an awful thing dealing with a man like Winston who is at the same moment dictatorial, eloquent and muddle-headed. I am not sure that I ever got into his mind that India pays for the whole of her defence including the British forces in India, or that there is no possible way of reducing these accumulating balances except by stopping to buy Indian goods or soldiers outside India.[98]

Amery continued on the theme of the weak-hearted response of the members of the Cabinet to Churchill's tirades on the Indian debt.

None of them ever really have the courage to stand up to Winston and tell him when he is making a fool of himself. Winston cannot see beyond such phrases as 'Are we to incur hundreds of millions of debt defending India in order to be kicked out by the Indians afterwards? This may be an ill-contrived world but not so ill-contrived as all that.'[99]

On the economic issue Amery believed that Churchill had stepped over the line into irrationality. At one stage he 'went off the deep end in a state of frantic passion on the whole subject of the humiliation of being kicked out of

97. Ibid.
98. Ibid., p. 836.
99. Ibid.

India by the beastliest people in the world next to the Germans.'[100]

By mid-1943 the adverse sterling balances had grown to the extent that whenever the question was raised there would be a 'Winstonian volcano' (which continued to be the case until the end of the war when the amount totalled £1,300 million, more than seventeen times the annual revenue of the Government of India and nearly one fifth of Britain's gross national product).[101] At one Cabinet meeting, 'Winston exploded for some twenty minutes to begin with and continued exploding and rumbling for the next two hours.' The essence of his argument was a 'counter claim' against the Indians for having saved them in the war. Once again Amery resorted to basic analogies to demonstrate the absurdity of Churchill's proposal to make a public statement repudiating the sterling balances: 'It may be honourable or necessary to bilk your cabby when you get to the station, but I cannot see how it helps telling him through the window that you mean to bilk him when you get there.'[102]

On these issues Amery slowly won out. Churchill took interest in economic detail only sporadically, and he did not demonstrate stamina in applying his intellect to long-range planning. Amery commanded the resources of the bureaucracy to pursue detailed cases against him. To Amery the issue of the Indian debt in a sense was a question of honour; but the sterling balances also bound the two countries together in a way that shaped his vision of the future. Economic dependence might be reversed, but

100. Ibid., p. 842.

101. B. R. Tomlinson, *The Political Economy of the Raj 1914–1947* (London, 1979), p. 140.

102. *Diaries*, II, p. 901.

the relationship would perpetuate the political connection.

Amery also succeeded in checking Churchill's impulses on the question of the appointment of a new Viceroy. Linlithgow had been in India for six years and had reached the end of his term of office. Churchill's choice in late 1942 was Sir Miles Lampson (soon to be Lord Killearn), the Ambassador in Egypt. During his tenure in Cairo, Lampson had provided, in Churchill's view, an admirable example of the way Britain's position of Imperial supremacy should be asserted. Lampson was a relic of a previous age, one of the last Proconsuls who bears comparison with Lord Cromer or Lord Curzon. In China, Lampson earlier had renegotiated the 'unequal treaties'. In Egypt, he was the architect of the Treaty of 1936, the legal basis of Britain's presence in the Canal Zone. He believed in the pomp and prestige of the British Empire. He seldom hesitated to intervene in Egyptian politics, with the threat of force if necessary, to maintain the British position. Churchill believed he had done a useful piece of work in early 1942 by imposing a more friendly regime in Cairo and thereby humiliating King Farouk.

Linlithgow as well as Amery believed that Lampson would be an unmitigated disaster as Viceroy. Amery's first choice was Sir Samuel Hoare, Churchill's old adversary in the battle of the India Act of 1935. Churchill would not give the suggestion of Hoare a second thought.[103] The debate between Churchill and Amery over alternative candidates took place on odd occasions, once for example when the former emerged from his bath and caused Amery to reflect that he was 'a very different figure from the little

---

103. Amery later raised Hoare's name again 'but on this Winston was adamant. The public had never yet forgiven him [for the] Hoare-Laval [pact] and Munich.' Amery MS Diary, 9 June 1943.

boy I first saw in a similar state of nature at Ducker fifty odd years ago!'[104] At one point Churchill suggested Harold Macmillan but immediately retracted the idea because he was too 'unstable'.[105] Amery viewed with favour the notion that Anthony Eden might make a good Viceroy and, as a further possibility, the leader of the Labour Party, Clement Attlee. Amery went so far as to broach the idea with Attlee himself ('God forbid', was Attlee's response.)[106] The more Amery thought about the question of the succession, the more he believed that his own sense of duty compelled him to put himself forward: '[F]ailing everybody else', he told Churchill on 30 November 1942, 'I . . . [am] prepared to go myself.' Amery was now sixty-nine years old. His age gave Churchill a ready excuse to decline the suggestion, but he gave another reason as well which Amery found ironic. By his association with Churchill, and by his own action in suppressing the 'Quit India' movement, Amery had acquired the reputation of a reactionary. If he were proposed as Viceroy, Churchill told him, 'it would be objected to both on the score of age and of my being a Diehard!!'[107]

No suitable candidate emerged. Linlithgow's term of office was therefore extended, even though Amery believed him to be 'stale' and 'near the end of his tether.'[108] The debate continued into the next year. In February 1943 Eden by general consensus moved into the position of probable Viceroy. 'I think he has courage', Amery wrote, 'and after Linlithgow his ease of manner and quickness

104. *Diaries*, II, p. 834.

105. Ibid., p. 846.

106. Amery MS Diary, 9 November 1942.

107. *Diaries*, II, p. 848; Amery to Churchill, 1 December 1942, Amery Papers.

108. Amery MS Diary, 3 December 1942.

of wit would make him very popular.'[109] Amery reflected that Eden might make a better Viceroy ruling in India than 'leading the nation here' as head of the Tories. He believed Eden to be deficient in areas of British social and economic policies. 'Anthony does not stand up to Winston because he . . . has so little in the way of a definite point of view.'[110] Thus there were good reasons for despatching Eden to Delhi, but Eden himself concluded that the Viceroyship would be a derailment on the route to the Prime Ministership. Churchill returned to the charge with 'the Egyptian menace', Amery's phrase for Lampson. Then on 9 June 1943 the decision tilted in favour of Field Marshal Sir Archibald Wavell.

As Amery's diary makes clear, Wavell became Viceroy by default. No better candidate could be found, but Churchill had an ulterior motive. He wished to relieve Wavell from military command—'to dispense with Wavell', as Amery put it in a communication to Linlithgow.[111] Linlithgow accepted the decision without enthusiasm. Amery, on the other hand, was convinced that Wavell was 'as good a solution as any.'[112] Behind the taciturn exterior, Wavell possessed a poet's temperament and a breadth of knowledge not usually associated with soldiers. Amery saw from the outset that Churchill had miscalculated and that 'Wavell may . . . prove more radical before long than most politicians.'[113]

109. Amery MS Diary, 25 February 1943.

110. Amery MS Diary, 7 May 1943.

111. Amery to Linlithgow, 'Private and Most Secret', 8 June 1943, in Mansergh, ed., *Transfer of Power*, III, p. 1048. 'You will have to become a civilian, and put off uniform', Churchill told Wavell. Moon, ed., *Wavell: The Viceroy's Journal*, p. 8.

112. *Diaries*, II, p. 892.

113. Amery MS Diary, 9 June 1943.

At the time of his appointment in mid-1943, Wavell had completed the second volume of his biography of Field Marshal Lord Allenby, who after the conquest of Jerusalem in the First World War had become High Commissioner in Egypt.[114] 'I am not sure', Amery wrote in his diary, 'whether Winston would have been so keen about Wavell as Viceroy if he had realised how thoroughly Wavell backs up Allenby's policy of sympathy with Egyptian nationalism.'[115] Wavell was pro-Arab and anti-Zionist, which brought him into direct conflict with Churchill. In India, Wavell immediately began to plan for independence. Churchill's intention in making the appointment had, of course, been the opposite. He had merely thought that Wavell as a former soldier would preserve the peace and keep an eye on the Indian Army. 'Winston has a curious hatred of India. . .', Amery wrote, 'and is convinced that the Indian Army is only waiting to shoot us in the back.'[116]

* * *

There were two final periods of confrontation between Amery and Churchill over India. The first was from mid-1943 until early 1945, when the friction continued as Amery attempted to persuade his colleagues in the Cabinet to endorse a plan for India's independence on VE or VJ Day. Failing to win support, Amery in the second and last phase threw his weight wholeheartedly behind Wavell's effort to reconcile Congress and the Muslim League.

114. See Field-Marshal Viscount Wavell of Cyrenaica and Winchester, *Allenby in Egypt: Being Volume II of Allenby: A Study in Greatness* (London, 1943).

115. *Diaries*, II, p. 896.

116. Amery MS Diary, 21 June 1943.

The tension between Amery and Churchill now mounted to the point of ultimate explosion.

Churchill at first believed that Amery had proselytized Wavell. In fact Amery was a restraining influence. Wavell, having received a political appointment, plunged headlong into Indian politics on the assumption that Indians of all convictions would follow the British lead if it came from the heart. He sympathized with Indian national aspirations. Amery's own proclivities were of course similar, but he tempered Wavell's optimism. Churchill suspected the opposite. 'Not unnaturally', Amery wrote, Churchill ' . . . thinks that I have been putting Wavell up to all of this whereas it is rather Wavell who has insisted on pushing forward his view'.[117] Churchill's new Indian appointments, which had been made on grounds on military expediency, were backfiring. For the same reason that he had elevated Wavell to the Viceroyship, he had appointed Field Marshal Sir Claude Auchinleck to Wavell's old post as Commander-in-Chief India.[118] Auchinleck was pro-Indian Army to the bone. When Churchill discovered his mistake, it made a lasting impression. 'That ass Wavell and that traitor Auchinleck', he later remarked to Amery.[119] This was strong language, but it summed up Churchill's sentiment during the last part of the war.

At the time of the new Viceroy's initiation into Churchill's Indian diatribes, Amery passed a note across the Cabinet table to Wavell that the Prime Minister 'knows

117. Amery MS Diary, 6 October 1943.

118. Churchill thus made room for the appointment of Lord Louis Mountbatten as Supreme Commander, South-East Asia. Amery had first made the suggestion that Mountbatten should have the job: 'Mountbatten told me at the outset that Winston had said to him that this was my idea and that he had not liked it at first, but had gradually come round to it.' *Diaries*, II, pp. 934 and 936.

119. Amery MS Diary, 30 September 1946.

as much of the Indian problem as George III did of the American colonies.'[120] The theme of an eventual revolt in India comparable to the American Revolution was a real anxiety on the part of Amery caused in part by Churchill's extravagant statements. Churchill had a penchant for rhetoric as a substitute for action of any sort in India, and the rhetoric itself Amery regarded as romantic, false, and dangerous. On one occasion Churchill in a typical outburst exclaimed that India's national regeneration could take place only by 'extinguishing landlords and oppressive industrialists' and by uplifting the peasants and untouchables. How this social revolution would be accomplished was never made clear or argued persuasively. Churchill took as another persistent theme the Indian debt, which would result in impoverished British workers who in turn would enrich Indian mill-owners. He even challenged Amery's patriotism by asking him why he did not stand up for his own countrymen against Indian moneylenders. At this provocation Amery lost his temper. But he made it clear that he drew a distinction between Churchill on India and Churchill as a wartime leader:

Naturally I lost patience and couldn't help telling him that I didn't see much difference between his outlook and Hitler's which annoyed him no little.

I am by no means sure whether on this subject of India he is really quite sane—there is no relation between his manner, physical and intellectual, on this theme and the equability and dominant good sense he displays on issues directly affecting the conduct of the war.[121]

120. Moon, ed., *Wavell: The Viceroy's Journal*, p. 12.
121. *Diaries*, II, p. 993.

Not sane on India but a great war leader—this was Amery's considered judgement.

Even before October 1943, Churchill had become alarmed at the new Viceroy's aim to bring Indian leaders together for discussion of ways for getting off dead centre. Churchill responded to Wavell's proposed course of action, in Amery's description, with 'irrelevant' discourses 'on the worthlessness and probable disloyalty of India's large and well-equipped army.'[122] Rather than give Wavell specific instructions, Churchill harangued him. 'You are wafted to India on a wave of hot air', Amery told Wavell on his departure.[123]

Wavell arrived in the midst of the Bengal famine. He began to 'badger' Churchill, in the latter's phrase, for grain shipments to relieve the catastrophe brought about by the capture of the rice-growing areas of South-East Asia by the Japanese. The causes of the famine itself were complex, described by Amery as 'general economic overstrain of which the famine is only a symptom.' Apart from the human suffering and actual starvation, Amery feared an economic collapse that would interfere with India's war effort.[124] Churchill responded to the entreaties of Wavell and Amery in typical style: despite the famine, Indians would continue to breed 'like rabbits'. Only by pressing

122. Ibid., p. 946.

123. Moon, ed., *Wavell: The Viceroy's Journal*, p. 23.

124. On the famine, see especially M. S. Venkataramani, *Bengal Famine of 1943* (Delhi, 1973). Venkataramani quotes from an American publication sympathetic to the plight of the Indians caught in the famine, *Amerasia*: 'The apparent acquiescence of the United States Government in British policy in this matter will increase the disillusionment and suspicion which many Indians already feel over what seems to them a readiness on the part of American authorities to follow obediently in the steps of the Secretary of State for India, Mr Amery.' (p. 47) Amery would have wryly noted the degree of control over American policy attributed to him.

the issue to the point of resignation did Wavell manage, with Amery's support, to obtain grain shipments. As a consequence Churchill believed that Wavell had proved himself to be 'the greatest failure as a Viceroy that we had ever had!'[125] Amery's assessment of Churchill was just as severe. 'India, or any form of self-government for coloured peoples, raises in him a wholly uncontrollable complex.'[126]

Amery's growing conviction—that Churchill was to India as George III had been to the American colonies—led him to formulate a plan to avert a revolutionary situation. 'The real difficulty with India', he explained to his colleagues in the India Committee of the Cabinet, 'was her subordination to this country. It was the same feeling that had resulted in the revolt of the American colonies.'[127] Amery's plan was bold in its imaginative simplicity. It was, as he described it, the inversion of the Cripps offer to grant India independence after the Indians themselves had agreed upon a constitution. In reversing the sequence, Amery now proposed to make a unilateral declaration that India would acquire 'full and unqualified independence within the Commonwealth on VE Day' (sometimes he suggested VJ Day instead). He was virtually alone among his colleagues in holding that the Indians were capable of managing their own affairs and in believing that they would respond to British magnanimity in a manner similar to the Afrikaners after the Boer War. He presented the proposal to the India Committee in a comment that ran to some 6,000 words. He put the final touches on the plan

125. Amery MS Diary, 5 November 1943.

126. *Diaries*, II, p. 988.

127. India Committee, 28 February 1945, in Mansergh, ed., *Transfer of Power*, V, p. 620.

on Christmas Day 1944. '[D]aring but really cautious and practical policy', he wrote in summing up his 'revolutionary' proposal.[128]

Amery made no headway at all. His only supporter turned out to be Sir Stafford Cripps. Since Amery had been a party to sabotaging Cripps's mission in 1942, the partnership was ironic. 'The ever useful Cripps', Amery remarked with gratitude in his diary. Cripps even defended Amery before Churchill, with whom, in the initial stages of the plan, Amery had his worst row yet. The immediate cause was again the financial debt, which Churchill blamed not only on Amery but also on Wavell 'for betraying this country's interests in order to curry favour with the Indians.' Amery responded in kind:

> I held on to myself for some time but could not help in the end exploding violently and telling him to stop talking damned nonsense. So the sparks flew for some minutes before he subsided and business continued.
>
> At the end of the meeting I told Winston I was sorry if I had used strong language but wished that he would ever find time to talk to me about these matters and find out how they really stood. It is terrible to think that in nearly five years, apart from incidental talks about appointments etc he has never once discussed either the Indian situation generally or this sterling balance question with me, but has only indulged in wild and indeed scarcely sane tirades in Cabinet.[129]

Amery wondered whether Churchill even stirred himself to read his proposal for India to achieve independence 'in

128. *Diaries*, II, pp. 1007 and 1023.
129. Ibid., p. 1018.

the hour of victory'.[130] The proposal itself failed to reach the Cabinet because it was attacked from all sides, not only by members of the India Committee but also by the Viceroy. Wavell believed that it would be fatal merely to proclaim independence and thus by-pass Jinnah, Gandhi, and the Congress leaders.[131] 'You had better drop it, Leo', John Simon (now Lord Chancellor) wrote in a note that signified the end to Amery's bid to make India independent at the end of the war.[132]

Amery encountered fierce opposition to his VE-VJ Day project in part because his plan would have yielded the initiative in setting the terms of independence to the various parties in India including the Congress, the Muslim League, and the Princes. The Indians might have, or they might not have, accepted the Westminster model as the basis of the constitution. There was the possibility, at least, that India might have entered the Commonwealth as an autocracy, which made the proposal unacceptable to Attlee and others who were committed to a Westminster-type solution. The implications were far reaching. Had Amery's proposal been accepted, the Commonwealth

130. Ibid., p. 1040. Amery later wrote: 'I doubt if he ever even saw my Xmas 1944 memorandum recommending immediate Dominion status for India on VJ Day.' Amery MS Diary, 3 June 1947.

131. Wavell also wrote: 'It seems to me quite unworkable, both for constitutional and psychological reasons. S[ecretary]. of S]tate]. has a curious capacity for getting hold of the right stick but practically always the wrong end of it.' Moon, ed., *Wavell: The Viceroy's Journal*, p. 111. On the other hand, H. V. Hodson, who saw the problem from the perspective of a former constitutional adviser to the Viceroy, wrote in *The Great Divide*, p. 117: 'It [the Amery plan] might conceivably have provided a solution that would have avoided all the struggles and calamities of the next three years and bequeathed a united India when the British departed.'

132. 'Everyone [was] against me, including my own advisers and Wavell.' *Diaries*, II, p. 1031.

might have evolved on different lines from those resulting from the 'one man, one vote' principle that became the basis of Commonwealth membership.

After Amery failed to make headway with his own plan, he closed ranks with Wavell. In the teeth of Churchill's opposition, Amery backed Wavell's proposal to return to London to argue for a conference of Indian leaders who in concert might be able to break the deadlock. Churchill eventually, but acrimoniously, acquiesced: 'he spoke most bitterly and contemptuously of W[avell] as never any real use as a soldier but who he thought would at least carry on in India and not try and advertise himself by cringing to the Hindus.'[133] After Wavell arrived in London he wrote about the proceedings of the India Committee that Amery supported him 'manfully and quite skilfully.'[134] Wavell nevertheless was occasionally dismayed at Amery's foibles in Cabinet discussion. 'Leo can never make a point and leave it at that, he always over-elaborates . . . he can never leave well enough alone.'[135] Amery for his part noted that Churchill was 'more hopelessly garrulous and time wasting than ever.' 'As usual', Amery continued, 'he poured contempt on Wavell and talked rubbish about abolishing landlords and money-lenders'.[136] Thus in late April 1945 Churchill and Wavell came to the breaking point. Amery made it clear that if Churchill forced the Viceroy's resignation, he would also resign. It is much to Amery's credit that he stuck with Wavell

133. Amery MS Diary, 16 March 1945.
134. Moon, ed., *Wavell: The Viceroy's Journal*, p. 126.
135. Ibid., pp. 134–35.
136. *Diaries*, II, p. 1039.

under Churchill's unremitting attacks.[137] Wavell, like Amery, was a man of honour. In the historical record, he and Amery emerge well in the encounter with the Prime Minister. It should also be reiterated, however, that the bitterness of the Indian dispute never diminished Amery's admiration for Churchill as a war leader.

The end of the story took an unexpected twist because of the sudden termination of the war. Immediately deciding that it would not do himself or the Tories any good if India became an issue in the British election, Churchill grew as friendly to Wavell as he previously had been hostile. Wavell returned to India to convene the Simla conference, which he regarded as a last-ditch effort to reconcile the Muslim League and Congress. It ended in failure. Neither Wavell nor Amery had any doubt that Jinnah's intransigence wrecked the chances for Indian unity, which might have succeeded if—a large if—the British had pressed forward earlier. 'The immediate wrecker was Jinnah', Amery wrote, 'but the real wrecker . . . [was] Winston.'[138]

* * *

It is useful to view Amery's ideas on India in the context of the British Empire, England, and the world in the twentieth century. Throughout his career he was consistent on the issue of national freedom. 'Unity in the last resort', he once wrote to Lionel Curtis, 'depends upon ideas and

137. In October 1944, Henry Channon (a Conservative MP and perceptive diarist) had recorded that Amery gave the impression of being 'terrified' of Churchill. (Robert Rhodes James, ed., *Chips: The Diaries of Sir Henry Channon* [London, 1967], p. 396) Whatever the impression may have been, the record shows that in Cabinet discussions Amery was one of Churchill's most tenacious critics.

138. *Diaries*, II, p. 1045. 'It was most disappointing that our efforts failed in the end', Wavell wrote to Amery. 22 July 1945, Amery Papers.

ideals and no [constitutional] machinery will keep together people who do not agree.'[139] Amery stands in British Imperial history as heir to the traditions of Joseph Chamberlain and Alfred Milner. As an intellectual of All Souls and as a statesman he held a vision of Imperial destiny for his country. He was a man of undisputed integrity, one of the reasons his voice counted in the downfall of the Chamberlain government. In the affairs of the British Empire his greatest achievement was progressively to expand his vision beyond the white Dominions to prepare the way for the transfer of power in India, thereby contributing to national independence elsewhere in Asia and eventually in Africa.

Hugh Dalton, who was President of the Board of Trade during the last part of the Second World War, once made a perceptive remark about Amery as Secretary of State for India and Churchill as Prime Minister: 'Amery—as many outside would be surprised to find—is always in Cabinet the warmest advocate of a "sympathic" and "constructive" policy in India, but is overborne by the P.M. . . .'[140] Sometimes the verbal and written exchanges were acerbic. But the negative aspects must not be allowed to overshadow the mutual respect. Amery believed that Churchill saved England in 1940–45 and that no one else could have done it. For his part, Churchill on Amery's death in 1955 described him with heart-felt emotion as 'a great patriot'.

---

139. Amery to Curtis, 2 October 1943, Curtis Papers, MS Curtis 28.

140. Ben Pimlott, ed., *The Second World War Diary of Hugh Dalton 1940–45* (London, 1986), p. 777.

Index

181

Index

Churchill, Winston Spencer (*cont.*)
pire, 45, agrees with Amery that
League of Nations and United Nations have no business meddling in
affairs of British Empire, 79,
shapes doctrine of Middle East
ruled by airplanes and armoured
cars, 82, on National Home good
for the Jews, good for the Arabs,
good for the British, and good for
the world, 82, pro T.E. Lawrence,
82–83, described by Amery as
'Congenitally Little England', 89,
theory of economic absorbtive capacity in Palestine, 91, rules in favour of Palestine's partition, 93,
defends Amery as a man of 'great
knowledge and mental energy', 93
n.41, believes Kenya will develop
into 'a characteristically and distinctively British colony', 99, described by Amery as mid-
Victorian Free Trader, 104–05,
compared with Lloyd George,
105, describes results of Ottawa
Conference as 'Rottawa', 106,
Amery's practical joke on in
House of Commons debate, 110–
11, agrees with Amery on need
for rearmament, 119, states that
Amery is 'the only person' consistently sound in judgement in mid-
1930s, 119, 'fossilized in mind'
compared with Amery, 120 n.113,
offers Amery India Office 13 May
1940, 123, wishes to keep Amery
out of mainstream business of
war, 124, schoolboy boisterousness
of, 124, wishes to have War Cabinet comply with his wishes, 125,
suspects Amery of Cabinet intrigue, 125–26, on Amery, Macmillan, Boothby, and P.J. Grigg
as instigators of Cabinet plot, 126
n.8, regards Amery's views on India's future as heresy, 127, ideas
on Gandhi reinforced by George
Lloyd and P.J. Grigg, 128 n.12,
his anti-Gandhi sentiment, 129,
views India as reservoir of manpower, 130, explodes in anger

over Amery's 1940 policy, 130, ac-
cuses Amery of stirring up revolution in India, 131, 133, sees no
connection between South African
and Indian issues, 131, alleges that
Amery has misled Cabinet, 132,
attacks Amery in Cabinet, 132,
reads Amery's correspondence
with Linlithgow and is 'a good
deal perturbed', 133, redrafts
statement promising Indian independence after war, 134, instransi-
gent towards Amery despite
Halifax's intervention, 134 n.22,
glad that Indians reject 'jolly good
offer', 135, accepts substance of
Amery's proposals, 135–36, writes
to Amery that 1940 incident is
closed, 136, shows 1940 correspondence to Anthony Eden to
prove that Amery has cast away
India, 136, convinced by Halifax
that Amery is more fool than
knave, 136 n.30, comments on
growing cleavage between Muslim
League and Congress, 'Oh, but
that is all to the good', 140, pon-
ders fate of India 1942, 144, and
Atlantic Charter, 145, 147–49, did
he see 'the true nakedness of the
land'?, 149 n.61, at heart still a
Free Trader, 147, does not intend
Atlantic Charter to be applied to
British Empire, 148, does not con-
sult Amery, 149, wishes to fly out
to India 1942 to steady nerves,
151, prepared to bargain with
'Hindoo Priesthood', 151, agrees
to send Cripps to India, 152, described by Amery as gaga, 157,
perturbed at giving up diehard position merely 'to secure more
American, Chinese, and Left
Wing support', 158, undermines
Cripps's position, 161, in 1942
looks upon Amery as 'a steady
and supporting influence and not
as a dangerous innovator!', 162,
row with Amery over Indian sterling balances, 164–66, 'an ill-
contrived world but not so ill-